Annotated Checklist
of the Birds of Belize

Bieuille
Flets 8-06
San Pedro Cat
Belize

Annotated Checklist
of the Birds of Belize

H. Lee Jones
&
A. C. Vallely

Lynx Edicions

Cover: Tody Motmot *Hylomanes momotula*, Andrew C. Vallely 2000.

First published: 2001

© **Lynx Edicions** - Passeig de Gràcia, 12, 08007 Barcelona, Spain
e-mail: lynx@hbw.com. *Web*: www.hbw.com

Printed and bound by S.A. de Litografía, Barcelona, Spain.
ISBN: 84-87334-35-0
D.L.: B-39375-2001

CONTENTS

INTRODUCTION

A great deal of new information on the Belize avifauna has accumulated since Stephen Russell published his landmark monograph *A distributional study of the birds of British Honduras* in 1964. Russell recognized a total of 465 species as definitely occurring in Belize. In 1986, Wood *et al.* published *A checklist of the birds of Belize* in which they listed 533 species. In 1994, Garcia *et al.* published an updated checklist which recognized 556 species, and in 1998, Miller and Miller published a checklist with the number of species reduced to 540. In 2000, they published a revised list with 549 species. The authors of these checklists have varied widely in their determinations of which species to accept for inclusion, and none since Russell have applied rigorous criteria for acceptance (Jones 2002).

The purpose of this checklist is to provide information on the status, abundance and habitats of the 566 species which we believe have been adequately documented as occurring in Belize. We still have much to learn about the habitats, geographic distribution, and relative abundances of birds in Belize. By publishing this list, it is our desire to elicit feedback from those who use it. In turn, we hope to update the list periodically as new information accumulates.

HOW TO USE THIS CHECKLIST

The first column lists scientific and English names in accordance with the sequence and nomenclature of the American Ornithologists Union (1998, 2000). Numbers in superscript following some English names refer the reader to the footnotes which provide additional information, including references to published accounts. The second column lists the habitats in which one should expect to find the species. Specific habitats are presented as two- or three-letter codes. These codes appear in upper case, (a species' primary habitat) or lower case, (secondary habitat). The remaining eight columns present the species' relative abundance and seasonal status in each of the six political districts, Ambergris Caye, and the other cayes collectively.

Readers should note that a species' relative abundance designation within each district applies only to its preferred habitat which, in turn, may be very limited. For example, Common Bush-Tanager and Blue-gray Tanager are both listed as vP (very common permanent resident) in Cayo, Stann Creek, and Toledo districts. However, the bush-tanager is restricted to sub-montane broadleaf forest, a habitat that is found only at higher elevations in the Maya Mountains. The Blue-gray Tanager, on the other hand, is a widespread resident of a number of open and disturbed habitats where birders are much more likely to be afield.

The term "local" (l) is used when a species is found in a district only in one to a few localities with appropriate habitat. For example, lowland pine forest is found in a narrow, north-south band the length of Stann Creek District, but the Rusty Sparrow is restricted to the southern portion (thus its designation lP). In Toledo District, however, it is common in pine forest wherever it occurs (thus its designation cP), even though pines in Toledo are limited to the northeastern fourth of the district. Several species (e.g., Lesser Scaup) are found regularly in wetland and open water habitats at Crooked Tree Wildlife Sanctuary but are scarce or absent in other similar areas. Also, many species (e.g., Tropical Kingbird) have become established on one or two cayes but not on many others with similar habitat. These are also designated with an "l" in the "other cayes" column.

Question marks may mean one of several things. A box with only a "?" indicates that the species is not definitely recorded in that district. A "?" between the abundance code and the seasonality code or in place of the abundance code indicates that the species' relative abundance in that district is uncertain or not known. A "?" after the seasonality code means that the seasonal status of the species is uncertain.

ACKNOWLEDGMENTS

The authors wish to thank Elizabeth Mallory, Nick Brokaw, Valerie Giles, and Guy Tudor, all of whom reviewed and commented on an early draft of this checklist. Jan Meerman generously provided data and assistance in developing the maps, and Mallory spent many hours modifying Meerman's vegetation map to more accurately reflect avian habitat types. Tam Nguyen provided invaluable assistance with the political/locality map. Paul Sweet provided information on material at The American Museum of Natural History. Many people provided the authors with extensive locality and seasonal data from their field notes. Foremost among these were Philip Balderamos, Dorothy and Jim Beveridge, Marcus England, Susan Lala, Ellen McRae, Martin Meadows, and Sam Tillett. Still others (see footnote credits) provided records of unusual occurrences, some of which are not yet published. A. C. V. is indebted to the staff of Manomet Observatory for Conservation Sciences and Programme for Belize for their generous help in his field work. Albert Martínez Vilalta of Lynx Edicions made several helpful suggestions and displayed great patience through our numerous updates and revisions.

KEY TO SYMBOLS

Column Headings

CO = Corozal District
OW = Orange Walk District
BE = Belize District
CA = Cayo District
SC = Stann Creek District
TO = Toledo District
AC = Ambergris Caye
OC = other cayes

Abundance

v = very common (10 or more/day on average)
c = common (1-10/day on average)
f = fairly common (seen on most but not all days)
u = uncommon (seen several times a year or season)
r = rare (present, but seldom seen — with P, S, and W)
o = occasional (not seen every year — with V, T, and W)
l = uncommon or even common locally, but absent or scarce in most of the district
m = marginally occurs in district

Seasonality

P = permanent resident (breeding either documented or assumed)
S = seasonal resident only (breeding documented or assumed)
V = visitor (non-migratory birds that do not breed in the district)
T = transient (migratory birds that neither breed nor spend the winter in the district)
W = winter resident (migratory birds that typically spend the winter in the district)
X = known from only one or two records

Habitats

Forested Habitats (including forest edge)

BFM/bfm = submontane broadleaf forest (Maya Mountains)
BFL/bfl = lowland broadleaf forest (includes high second growth)
PFM/pfm = submontane pine forest (Mountain Pine Ridge)
PFL/pfl = lowland pine forest
MF/mf = mangrove and littoral forest

Transitional Habitats

SC/sc = scrub, low second growth
SA/sa = savanna (pine, oak, calabash, palmetto)

Unforested Habitats

AG/ag = cultivated land, pastureland, fallow fields, ornamental/landscaped vegetation (parks, towns, villages)
WL/wl = wetland habitats with emergent vegetation (sedge savannas, wet meadows, marshes, ricefields)
LA/la = lagoons, ponds, rivers, streams
BE/be = beaches, sandflats, mudflats, aquaculture farms
OC/oc = ocean

Habitats		Corozal District	Orange Walk District	Belize District	Cayo District	Stann Creek District	Toledo District	Ambergris Caye	other cayes

TINAMIFORMES

TINAMIDAE (Tinamous)									(4)
Tinamus major GREAT TINAMOU	BFM,BFL pfm,pfl,sc	?P	fP	uP	fP	fP	fP		
Crypturellus soui LITTLE TINAMOU	SC bfm,bfl,pfm,pfl	?P	fP	fP	fP	fP	fP		
Crypturellus cinnamomeus THICKET TINAMOU	BFL,SC	cP	fP	lP	lP				
Crypturellus boucardi SLATY-BREASTED TINAMOU	BFM,BFL		fP	mP?	fP	fP	fP		

PODICIPEDIFORMES

PODICIPEDIDAE (Grebes)									(2)
Tachybaptus dominicus LEAST GREBE	WL,LA	lP	lP	uP	lP	lP	lP		
Podilymbus podiceps PIED-BILLED GREBE	WL,LA	lW	lW	lP	lW	lW	lP		

PROCELLARIIFORMES

PROCELLARIIDAE (Shearwaters)									(2)
Puffinus puffinus MANX SHEARWATER[1]	OC					X			
Puffinus lherminieri AUDUBON'S SHEARWATER[2]	OC					X			X

PELECANIFORMES

PHAETHONTIDAE (Tropicbirds)									(1)
Phaethon lepturus WHITE-TAILED TROPICBIRD[3]	OC								X

SULIDAE (Boobies)									(3)
Sula dactylatra MASKED BOOBY[4]	OC			X				X	X

Forested Habitats: BFM/bfm = submontane broadleaf forest; BFL/bfl = lowland broadleaf forest; PFM/pfm = submontane pine forest; PFL/pfl = lowland pine forest; MF/mf = mangrove and littoral forest.
Transitional Habitats: SC/sc = scrub, low second growth; SA/sa = savanna.
Unforested Habitats: AG/ag = cultivated land, pastureland, ornamental vegetation; WL/wl = wetland habitats with emergent vegetation ; LA/la = lagoons, ponds, rivers, streams; BE/be = coastal habitats; OC/oc = ocean.

	Habitats	Corozal District	Orange Walk District	Belize District	Cayo District	Stann Creek District	Toledo District	Ambergris Caye	other cayes
Sula leucogaster BROWN BOOBY	MF,OC			oV		oV	oV	oV	fV
Sula sula RED-FOOTED BOOBY	MF,OC			X				oV	IP

PELECANIDAE (Pelicans)									(2)
Pelecanus erythrorhynchos AMERICAN WHITE PELICAN[5]	LA,BE wl	IW	X	IW	X	IW	IW	X	X
Pelecanus occidentalis BROWN PELICAN	MF,BE,OC	cP	oV	vV	oV	vV	vV	✓P	vP

PHALACROCORACIDAE (Cormorants)									(2)
Phalacrocorax brasilianus NEOTROPIC CORMORANT	LA,BE oc	cP	cP	vP	fP	cP	cP	oP✓	IV
Phalacrocorax auritus DOUBLE-CRESTED CORMORANT	MF,BE la	cV	rV	cV		IV	uV	cP	cV

ANHINGIDAE (Anhingas)									(1)
Anhinga anhinga ANHINGA	LA mf	fP	fP	fP	uP	fP	fP	rP	oV

FREGATIDAE (Frigatebirds)									(1)
Fregata magnificens MAGNIFICENT FRIGATEBIRD	MF,BE,OC	cP	oV	vV	oV	vV	vV	✓P	vP

CICONIIFORMES

ARDEIDAE (Bitterns, Herons, and Egrets)									(16)
Botaurus pinnatus PINNATED BITTERN	WL		rP	rP	IP		IP?		
Botaurus lentiginosus AMERICAN BITTERN	WL		oW	X	X		X		
Ixobrychus exilis LEAST BITTERN	WL	rP?	rP?	rP?	X			oT	oT
Tigrisoma mexicanum BARE-THROATED TIGER-HERON	WL,LA	uP	fP	fP	uP	uP	uP	rP	

Key simbols:
Abundance: v = very common; c = common; f = fairly common; u = uncommon; r = rare; o = occasional; l = uncommon or even common locally, but absent or scarce in most of the district; m = marginally occurs in district.
Seasonality: P = permanent resident; S = seasonal resident only; V = visitor; T = transient; W = winter resident; X = known from only one or two records.

Habitats		Corozal District	Orange Walk District	Belize District	Cayo District	Stann Creek District	Toledo District	Ambergris Caye	other cayes
Ardea herodias GREAT BLUE HERON	WL,LA,BE mf	cP	cV	cV	fV	cV	cV	cP	uV
Ardea alba GREAT EGRET	WL,LA,BE mf	vP	vV	vP	cV	vV	vP		uV
Egretta thula SNOWY EGRET	WL,LA,BE mf	vP	vV	vP	cV	vV	vV	vP	uV
Egretta caerulea LITTLE BLUE HERON	MF,WL,LA,BE	vW	vW	vW	vW	vW	vW		cW
Egretta tricolor TRICOLORED HERON	MF,LA,BE wl	cP	fV	cV	uV	cV	cV	cP	uP
Egretta rufescens REDDISH EGRET	MF,BE	uP	X	uV		IV	IV	uP	IV
Bubulcus ibis CATTLE EGRET	AG mf,wl	vW	vW	vP	vW	vW	vW	cW	fT
Butorides virescens GREEN HERON	MF,LA,BE wl	cP	cV	cP	cV	cV	cV	cP	cP
Agamia agami AGAMI HERON	LA	?	uP	uP	rP	rP	rP		
Nycticorax nycticorax BLACK-CROWNED NIGHT-HERON	LA wl	fW	uW	fW	uW	uW	uW	oT	X
Nyctanassa violacea YELLOW-CROWNED NIGHT-HERON	MF,LA ag,wl	cP	cP	cP	uP	cP	cP	cP	cP
Cochlearius cochlearius BOAT-BILLED HERON	MF,LA	fP	fP	fP	uP	IP	IP	rP	IP

THRESKIORNITHIDAE (Ibises and Spoonbills) (4)

Habitats		Corozal District	Orange Walk District	Belize District	Cayo District	Stann Creek District	Toledo District	Ambergris Caye	other cayes
Eudocimus albus WHITE IBIS	MF,LA,BE wl	cP	IP	cP		fP	fP	uP	uV
Eudocimus ruber SCARLET IBIS[6]	MF,LA					X			
Plegadis falcinellus GLOSSY IBIS[7]	WL,LA	?	IW	IW	X	X	X		
Ajaia ajaja ROSEATE SPOONBILL	LA,BE mf,wl	fP	uV	fV	?	uV	uV	uP	oV

Forested Habitats: BFM/bfm = submontane broadleaf forest; BFL/bfl = lowland broadleaf forest; PFM/pfm = submontane pine forest; PFL/pfl = lowland pine forest; MF/mf = mangrove and littoral forest.
Transitional Habitats: SC/sc = scrub, low second growth; SA/sa = savanna.
Unforested Habitats: AG/ag = cultivated land, pastureland, ornamental vegetation; WL/wl = wetland habitats with emergent vegetation ; LA/la = lagoons, ponds, rivers, streams; BE/be = coastal habitats; OC/oc = ocean.

13

Habitats	Corozal District	Orange Walk District	Belize District	Cayo District	Stann Creek District	Toledo District	Ambergris Caye	other cayes
CICONIIDAE (Storks)								(2)
Jabiru mycteria JABIRU	SA,LA,BE wl	IP	IP	IP	oV	IP	IP	X	
Mycteria americana WOOD STORK	LA,BE wl	cP	fV	fV	uV	uV	uP	IP	IP

Habitats								
CATHARTIDAE (Vultures)								(4)
Coragyps atratus BLACK VULTURE	SA,AG,BE wl	vP	vP	vP	vP	vP	vP	uV	X
Cathartes aura TURKEY VULTURE	SA,AG,BE wl	vP	vP	vP	vP	vP	vP	oV	X
Cathartes burrovianus LESSER YELLOW-HEADED VULTURE	SA,AG,BE wl	uP	fP	fP	IP	fP	fP	uV	
Sarcoramphus papa KING VULTURE	BFL,PFM,PFL,SC ag	oV	uP	uP	fP	uP	uP		

PHOENICOPTERIFORMES

Habitats								
PHOENICOPTERIDAE (Flamingos)								(1)
Phoenicopterus ruber GREATER FLAMINGO[8]	LA,BE	X	X	X		X			

ANSERIFORMES

Habitats								
ANATIDAE (Waterfowl)								(17)
Dendrocygna autumnalis BLACK-BELLIED WHISTLING-DUCK	WL la	u?P	cP	cP	IW	IW	IW		X
Dendrocygna bicolor FULVOUS WHISTLING-DUCK[9]	WL,LA		IW	IW	X			X	
Anser albifrons GREATER WHITE-FRONTED GOOSE[10]	AG,LA			X					
Chen coerulescens SNOW GOOSE[11]	AG,LA		X		X				
Cairina moschata MUSCOVY DUCK	LA wl	uP	uP	uP	IP	uP	uP		
Anas americana AMERICAN WIGEON[12]	WL,LA	uW	uW	uW	uW			X	

Key simbols:
Abundance: v = very common; c = common; f = fairly common; u = uncommon; r = rare; o = occasional; l = uncommon or even common locally, but absent or scarce in most of the district; m = marginally occurs in district.
Seasonality: P = permanent resident; S = seasonal resident only; V = visitor; T = transient; W = winter resident; X = known from only one or two records.

Habitats	Corozal District	Orange Walk District	Belize District	Cayo District	Stann Creek District	Toledo District	Ambergris Caye	other cayes
Anas platyrhynchos MALLARD[13] WL,LA				X				
Anas discors BLUE-WINGED TEAL WL,LA	cW	cW	cW	fW	cW	cW	fW	IT
Anas cyanoptera CINNAMON TEAL[14] WL,LA			X	X	X			
Anas clypeata NORTHERN SHOVELER[15] WL,LA		oW	uW	oW		oW	X	
Anas acuta NORTHERN PINTAIL WL,LA		oW	oW	X	oW			
Anas crecca GREEN-WINGED TEAL[16] WL,LA			X	oW	X			
Aythya collaris RING-NECKED DUCK[17] LA wl		oW	lW	X		X	X	
Aythya affinis LESSER SCAUP LA wl	cW	oW	lW		oW	X		oT
Lophodytes cucullatus HOODED MERGANSER[18] LA			X					
Mergus serrator RED-BREASTED MERGANSER[19] LA			X					X
Nomonyx dominicus MASKED DUCK[20] WL			rW	X				

FALCONIFORMES

ACCIPITRIDAE (Osprey, Kites, Harriers, Hawks, and Eagles) (31)

Habitats	Corozal District	Orange Walk District	Belize District	Cayo District	Stann Creek District	Toledo District	Ambergris Caye	other cayes
Pandion haliaetus OSPREY MF,LA,OC	fP	uP	fP	uP	fP	fP	fP	fP
Leptodon cayanensis GRAY-HEADED KITE BFM,BFL pfm	uP	uP	uP	uP	uP	uP		
Chondrohierax uncinatus HOOK-BILLED KITE BFM,BFL pfm	?P	uP	?P	uP	uP	uP	X	
Elanoides forficatus SWALLOW-TAILED KITE PFM,PFL bfm,bfl	uT	lS	uS	fS	fS	fS		X
Elanus leucurus WHITE-TAILED KITE AG,WL	fP	fP	fP	fP	fP	fP	oV	
Rostrhamus sociabilis SNAIL KITE WL,LA	fP	fP	fP	oV	uV	oV		
Harpagus bidentatus DOUBLE-TOOTHED KITE BFM,BFL	?	uP	?	uP	uP	uP	oV	

Forested Habitats: BFM/bfm = submontane broadleaf forest; BFL/bfl = lowland broadleaf forest; PFM/pfm = submontane pine forest; PFL/pfl = lowland pine forest; MF/mf = mangrove and littoral forest.
Transitional Habitats: SC/sc = scrub, low second growth; SA/sa = savanna.
Unforested Habitats: AG/ag = cultivated land, pastureland, ornamental vegetation; WL/wl = wetland habitats with emergent vegetation ; LA/la = lagoons, ponds, rivers, streams; BE/be = coastal habitats; OC/oc = ocean.

	Habitats	Corozal District	Orange Walk District	Belize District	Cayo District	Stann Creek District	Toledo District	Ambergris Caye	other cayes
Ictinia mississippiensis MISSISSIPPI KITE[21]	Aerial			X	X		oT		
Ictinia plumbea PLUMBEOUS KITE	BFL,PFM,PFL,SA sc	uS	uS	uS	uS	uS	uS		
Busarellus nigricollis BLACK-COLLARED HAWK	LA	uP	uP	uP	uP	rP			
Circus cyaneus NORTHERN HARRIER	AG,WL,LA	oW	oW	oW	oW	oW	oW		X
Accipiter striatus SHARP-SHINNED HAWK	BFM,BFL,PFM,PFL sc	oW	oW	oW	oW	oW	oW	oW	
Accipiter cooperii COOPER'S HAWK	BFM,BFL,PFM,PFL sc		oW	oW	oW	oW	oW		
Accipiter bicolor BICOLORED HAWK	BFM,BFL pfm	rP	rP	rP	rP	rP	rP		
Geranospiza caerulescens CRANE HAWK	BFL,PFL sc,sa	uP	uP	uP	uP	uP	rP	X	
Leucopternis albicollis WHITE HAWK	BFL pfm			uP	mP	uP	uP		
Asturina nitida GRAY HAWK	BFL,SC,AG sa	fP	fP	fP	fP	fP	fP	oV	
Buteogallus anthracinus COMMON BLACK-HAWK	MF,SC,AG wl,la	uP	uP	fP	uP	fP	fP	*(mark)*	lP
Buteogallus urubitinga GREAT BLACK-HAWK	BFM,BFL,LA sc,wl	uP	fP	uP	uP	uP	uP		
Harpyhaliaetus solitarius SOLITARY EAGLE[22]	BFM,PFM				rP	X	X		
Buteo magnirostris ROADSIDE HAWK	SC,SA,AG	cP	cP	cP	cP	cP	cP *(mark)*		
Buteo platypterus BROAD-WINGED HAWK	SC,AG bfl,pfm,pfl	X	X	X	oW	X	oT	X	X
Buteo brachyurus SHORT-TAILED HAWK[23]	BFM,BFL,PFM,PFL sc	fP	fP	fP	fP	fP	fP	oV	X
Buteo albicaudatus WHITE-TAILED HAWK	AG,SA	uP	uP	uP	uP	uP	lP		
Buteo albonotatus ZONE-TAILED HAWK	SA,AG,WL	?	oW	oW	oW	?	oW		
Buteo jamaicensis RED-TAILED HAWK	PFM bfm,bfl			X	uP	oV	X		
Morphnus guianensis CRESTED EAGLE[24]	BFL		rP				rP		

Key simbols:
Abundance: v = very common; c = common; f = fairly common; u = uncommon; r = rare; o = occasional; l = uncommon or even common locally, but absent or scarce in most of the district; m = marginally occurs in district.
Seasonality: P = permanent resident; S = seasonal resident only; V = visitor; T = transient; W = winter resident; X = known from only one or two records.

16

Habitats	Corozal District	Orange Walk District	Belize District	Cayo District	Stann Creek District	Toledo District	Ambergris Caye	other cayes
Harpia harpyja HARPY EAGLE[25] BFM,BFL				rP		rP		
Spizastur melanoleucus BLACK-AND-WHITE HAWK-EAGLE BFM,BFL		rP	rP	uP	rP	rP		
Spizaetus tyrannus BLACK HAWK-EAGLE BFM,BFL,PFM,PFL / sc	uP	uP	uP	uP	uP	uP		
Spizaetus ornatus ORNATE HAWK-EAGLE BFM,BFL / pfm,pfl		uP	rP	rP	rP	rP		

FALCONIDAE (Falcons) (10)

Habitats	Corozal District	Orange Walk District	Belize District	Cayo District	Stann Creek District	Toledo District	Ambergris Caye	other cayes
Micrastur ruficollis BARRED FOREST-FALCON BFM,BFL		fP	rP	uP	uP	uP		
Micrastur semitorquatus COLLARED FOREST-FALCON BFM,BFL,PFM,PFL / sc	uP	fP	fP	fP	fP	fP		
Caracara cheriway CRESTED CARACARA[26] SA,AG	?	X		?				
Herpetotheres cachinnans LAUGHING FALCON PFL,SC,SA	fP	fP	fP	fP	fP	fP	rP	
Falco sparverius AMERICAN KESTREL SA,AG	fW	fW	uW	uW	uW	uW	uW	uT
Falco columbarius MERLIN MF,LA,BE,OC / ag,wl,la	uW	oW	uW	oW	uW	uW	uW	uT
Falco femoralis APLOMADO FALCON SA / ag	oV	uP	uP	uP	uP	IP		
Falco rufigularis BAT FALCON SC,AG / bfl,pfl,sa	fP	fP	fP	fP	fP	fP	X	
Falco deiroleucus ORANGE-BREASTED FALCON BFM,PFM / bfl,pfl			X		IP	X	X	
Falco peregrinus PEREGRINE FALCON MF,LA,BE / ag,wl,la,oc	uW	uW	uW	uW	uW	uW	uW	fT

GALLIFORMES

CRACIDAE (Guans and Curassows) (3)

Habitats	Corozal District	Orange Walk District	Belize District	Cayo District	Stann Creek District	Toledo District	Ambergris Caye	other cayes
Ortalis vetula PLAIN CHACHALACA BFL,PFM,PFL,SC / bfm	cP	cP	cP	cP	cP	cP	uP	
Penelope purpurascens CRESTED GUAN BFM,BFL,PFM	uP	uP	IP	uP	uP	uP		
Crax rubra GREAT CURASSOW BFM,BFL	uP	uP	IP	uP	uP	uP		

Forested Habitats: BFM/bfm = submontane broadleaf forest; BFL/bfl = lowland broadleaf forest; PFM/pfm = submontane pine forest; PFL/pfl = lowland pine forest; MF/mf = mangrove and littoral forest.
Transitional Habitats: SC/sc = scrub, low second growth; SA/sa = savanna.
Unforested Habitats: AG/ag = cultivated land, pastureland, ornamental vegetation; WL/wl = wetland habitats with emergent vegetation ; LA/la = lagoons, ponds, rivers, streams; BE/be = coastal habitats; OC/oc = ocean.

	Habitats	Corozal District	Orange Walk District	Belize District	Cayo District	Stann Creek District	Toledo District	Ambergris Caye	other cayes
PHASIANIDAE (Turkeys)									(1)
Meleagris ocellata OCELLATED TURKEY	BFL,PFM		uP		uP				
ODONTOPHORIDAE (New World Quail)									(3)
Colinus nigrogularis BLACK-THROATED BOBWHITE	SA sc,ag	fP	fP	fP	mP	fP	mP		
Odontophorus guttatus SPOTTED WOOD-QUAIL	BFM,BFL pfm,pfl	?	uP	?	uP	uP	uP		
Dactylortyx thoracicus SINGING QUAIL[27]	BFL,SC		rP		rP	?		rP	

GRUIFORMES

	Habitats	Corozal District	Orange Walk District	Belize District	Cayo District	Stann Creek District	Toledo District	Ambergris Caye	other cayes
RALLIDAE (Rails, Gallinules, and Coots)									(13)
Laterallus ruber RUDDY CRAKE	AG wl	uP	fP	fP	fP	fP	cP	uP	
Laterallus exilis GRAY-BREASTED CRAKE[28]	AG,WL		rP?	X			IP		
Laterallus jamaicensis BLACK RAIL	WL			X	X	X	X		
Rallus longirostris CLAPPER RAIL	MF	IP		IP		uP	uP	fP	fP
Aramides axillaris RUFOUS-NECKED WOOD-RAIL	MF	?		rP		rP	rP	uP	IP
Aramides cajanea GRAY-NECKED WOOD-RAIL	AG,WL,LA sc	fP	fP	fP	fP	fP	fP		
Amaurolimnas concolor UNIFORM CRAKE	BFL		rP	rP	rP	rP	rP		
Porzana carolina SORA	WL	IW	IW	IW	IW	IW	IW	uT	uT
Porzana flaviventer YELLOW-BREASTED CRAKE[29]	WL			X	X				
Pardirallus maculatus SPOTTED RAIL	WL		IP	IP			X		
Porphyrula martinica PURPLE GALLINULE	WL,LA	IP	IP	IP	IP	IP	IP	X	X

Key simbols:
Abundance: v = very common; c = common; f = fairly common; u = uncommon; r = rare; o = occasional; l = uncommon or even common locally, but absent or scarce in most of the district; m = marginally occurs in district.
Seasonality: P = permanent resident; S = seasonal resident only; V = visitor; T = transient; W = winter resident; X = known from only one or two records.

Habitats	Corozal District	Orange Walk District	Belize District	Cayo District	Stann Creek District	Toledo District	Ambergris Caye	other cayes
Gallinula chloropus COMMON MOORHEN	WL,LA	uV	uP	uP	o?W	uW	IW	oT	oT
Fulica americana AMERICAN COOT	WL,LA	fW	IW	IW	IW	IW	IW		X

HELIORNITHIDAE (Finfoots) (1)

Habitats	Corozal District	Orange Walk District	Belize District	Cayo District	Stann Creek District	Toledo District	Ambergris Caye	other cayes
Heliornis fulica SUNGREBE	LA		uP	uP	uP	uP	uP		

ARAMIDAE (Limpkin) (1)

Habitats	Corozal District	Orange Walk District	Belize District	Cayo District	Stann Creek District	Toledo District	Ambergris Caye	other cayes
Aramus guarauna LIMPKIN	WL,LA ag	cP	cP	cP	uP	cP	cP	rP	

CHARADRIIFORMES

CHARADRIIDAE (Plovers) (7)

Habitats	Corozal District	Orange Walk District	Belize District	Cayo District	Stann Creek District	Toledo District	Ambergris Caye	other cayes
Pluvialis squatarola BLACK-BELLIED PLOVER	BE	uW		fW		uW	IW	uW	uW
Pluvialis dominica AMERICAN GOLDEN-PLOVER[30]	WL ag		IT	oT		IT			
Charadrius collaris COLLARED PLOVER[31]	BE			rP		X	rP?	X	oT
Charadrius alexandrinus SNOWY PLOVER[32]	BE			X					
Charadrius wilsonia WILSON'S PLOVER	BE	IV		IP		IP	IP	fP	oT
Charadrius semipalmatus SEMIPALMATED PLOVER	BE wl	IW	IT	fW		fW	IW	🖊	uW
Charadrius vociferus KILLDEER	AG,WL	fW	fW	fW	fW	fW	fW	🖊	uT

HAEMATOPODIDAE (Oystercatchers) (1)

Habitats	Corozal District	Orange Walk District	Belize District	Cayo District	Stann Creek District	Toledo District	Ambergris Caye	other cayes
Haematopus palliates AMERICAN OYSTERCATCHER[33]	BE			X		IW			X

Forested Habitats: BFM/bfm = submontane broadleaf forest; BFL/bfl = lowland broadleaf forest; PFM/pfm = submontane pine forest; PFL/pfl = lowland pine forest; MF/mf = mangrove and littoral forest.
Transitional Habitats: SC/sc = scrub, low second growth; SA/sa = savanna.
Unforested Habitats: AG/ag = cultivated land, pastureland, ornamental vegetation; WL/wl = wetland habitats with emergent vegetation ; LA/la = lagoons, ponds, rivers, streams; BE/be = coastal habitats; OC/oc = ocean.

Habitats	Corozal District	Orange Walk District	Belize District	Cayo District	Stann Creek District	Toledo District	Ambergris Caye	other cayes
RECURVIROSTRIDAE (Stilts and Avocets)								(2)
Himantopus mexicanus BLACK-NECKED STILT — WL,BE	cW	cW	IP	IW	fW	fW	uW	uT
Recurvirostra americana AMERICAN AVOCET[34] — WL,BE			oW			oT		

Habitats	Corozal District	Orange Walk District	Belize District	Cayo District	Stann Creek District	Toledo District	Ambergris Caye	other cayes
JACANIDAE (Jacanas)								(1)
Jacana spinosa NORTHERN JACANA — WL	cP	cP	cP	IP	IP	IP		

Habitats	Corozal District	Orange Walk District	Belize District	Cayo District	Stann Creek District	Toledo District	Ambergris Caye	other cayes
SCOLOPACIDAE (Sandpipers)								(26)
Tringa melanoleuca GREATER YELLOWLEGS — WL,BE	uW	fW	fW	oT	uW	uW	uW	uT
Tringa flavipes LESSER YELLOWLEGS — WL,BE	uW	fW	fW	oW	uW	uW	uW	uT
Tringa solitaria SOLITARY SANDPIPER — WL	fW	fW	fW	fW	fW	fW	uW	oT
Catoptrophorus semipalmatus WILLET — BE	uW	oW	uW		uW	IW	uW	oT
Actitis macularia SPOTTED SANDPIPER — MF,LA,BE	cW	cW	cW	fW	cW	cW		cW
Bartramia longicauda UPLAND SANDPIPER[35] — AG		X	X	X		X	X	X
Numenius phaeopus WHIMBREL — BE	?		uW		uT	oT	oT	oT
Numenius americanus LONG-BILLED CURLEW[36] — AG,BE / wl		X	?	X				X
Limosa haemastica HUDSONIAN GODWIT[37] — BE / wl			X		X			
Limosa fedoa MARBLED GODWIT[38] — BE / wl			X				X	X
Arenaria interpres RUDDY TURNSTONE — BE	uW		fW		fW	uW		cW
Calidris canutus RED KNOT — BE / wl			IW		IW			X
Calidris alba SANDERLING — BE	IW		uW		uW	IW		oT

Key simbols:
Abundance: v = very common; c = common; f = fairly common; u = uncommon; r = rare; o = occasional; l = uncommon or even common locally, but absent or scarce in most of the district; m = marginally occurs in district.
Seasonality: P = permanent resident; S = seasonal resident only; V = visitor; T = transient; W = winter resident; X = known from only one or two records.

Habitats		Corozal District	Orange Walk District	Belize District	Cayo District	Stann Creek District	Toledo District	Ambergris Caye	other cayes
Calidris pusilla SEMIPALMATED SANDPIPER[39]	WL,BE	?T	IT	IT	?T	IT	IT	uT	oT
Calidris mauri WESTERN SANDPIPER[40]	WL,BE	?W	IW	IW	?T	IW	IW	uW	uT
Calidris minutilla LEAST SANDPIPER	WL,BE	cW	cW	vW	u?W	vW	vW	cW	uT
Calidris fuscicollis WHITE-RUMPED SANDPIPER[41]	WL,BE	IT	cT	cT	IT	IT	IT	oT	oT
Calidris melanotos PECTORAL SANDPIPER	WL,BE	uT	fT	fT	?	fT	fT	uT	uT
Calidris alpina DUNLIN[42]	BE			X		X	X		
Calidris himantopus STILT SANDPIPER	WL		IW	uT		uT	uT	oT	
Tryngites subruficollis BUFF-BREASTED SANDPIPER	AG,WL		oT	X			oT		
Limnodromus griseus SHORT-BILLED DOWITCHER	WL	uW	IW	fW	IW	uW	uW	uT	uT
Limnodromus scolopaceus LONG-BILLED DOWITCHER[43]	WL	?	IW	IW	?	oW	oW	?	X
Gallinago gallinago COMMON SNIPE	WL	uW	uW	uW	uW	uW	uW	uW	uT
Phalaropus tricolor WILSON'S PHALAROPE[44]	WL,LA be			X		X	X		
Phalaropus lobatus RED-NECKED PHALAROPE[45]	LA,OC								X

LARIDAE (Jaegers, Gulls, Terns, and Skimmers)									(24)
Stercorarius skua GREAT SKUA[46]	OC			?				X	
Stercorarius pomarinus POMARINE JAEGER[47]	OC			oT		?		X	X
Stercorarius parasiticus PARASITIC JAEGER[47]	OC			oT		?		X	X
Larus atricilla LAUGHING GULL[48]	BE,OC	vV	cV	vV	X	vV	vV	vP	vP
Larus pipixcan FRANKLIN'S GULL[49]	LA,BE oc			oT			oT	X	X
Larus philadelphia BONAPARTE'S GULL[50]	LA,BE,OC		X	oW				X	

Forested Habitats: BFM/bfm = submontane broadleaf forest; BFL/bfl = lowland broadleaf forest; PFM/pfm = submontane pine forest; PFL/pfl = lowland pine forest; MF/mf = mangrove and littoral forest.
Transitional Habitats: SC/sc = scrub, low second growth; SA/sa = savanna.
Unforested Habitats: AG/ag = cultivated land, pastureland, ornamental vegetation; WL/wl = wetland habitats with emergent vegetation ; LA/la = lagoons, ponds, rivers, streams; BE/be = coastal habitats; OC/oc = ocean.

21

	Habitats	Corozal District	Orange Walk District	Belize District	Cayo District	Stann Creek District	Toledo District	Ambergris Caye	other cayes
Larus crassirostris BLACK-TAILED GULL[51]	BE,OC					X			
Larus delawarensis RING-BILLED GULL	BE,OC la	oW		oW		?	oW	oW	
Larus argentatus HERRING GULL	BE,OC	u?W	X	uW		oW	oW	uW	oW
Rissa tridactyla BLACK-LEGGED KITTIWAKE[52]	OC be								X
Sterna nilotica GULL-BILLED TERN	LA,BE	oW		uW		uW	oW	oW	X
Sterna caspia CASPIAN TERN	LA,BE	fW	X	fW		oW	oT	✏	X
Sterna maxima ROYAL TERN	BE,OC	cV		cV		cV	cV	cV	cV
Sterna sandvicensis SANDWICH TERN	BE,OC	vV	oV	vV		vV	vV	fV	fP
Sterna dougallii ROSEATE TERN	BE,OC					X			IS
Sterna hirundo COMMON TERN[53]	BE,OC	oW		oW		?	oW		uT
Sterna forsteri FORSTER'S TERN[54]	LA,BE oc	rW		rW		?	X	X	
Sterna antillarum LEAST TERN	BE,OC	IS		IS		IS	IS	uS	IS
Sterna anaethetus BRIDLED TERN	BE,OC							oV	fS
Sterna fuscata SOOTY TERN	BE,OC			X		X	X	oV	IS
Chlidonias niger BLACK TERN	LA,OC wl,be	?T	uT	cT		fT	fT	fT	cT
Anous stolidus BROWN NODDY	BE,OC						X		uV
Anous minutus BLACK NODDY[55]	BE,OC			X					X
Rynchops niger BLACK SKIMMER	LA,BE		X	oW		oW			X

Key simbols:
Abundance: v = very common; c = common; f = fairly common; u = uncommon; r = rare; o = occasional; l = uncommon or even common locally, but absent or scarce in most of the district; m = marginally occurs in district.
Seasonality: P = permanent resident; S = seasonal resident only; V = visitor; T = transient; W = winter resident; X = known from only one or two records.

COLUMBIFORMES

Habitats		Corozal District	Orange Walk District	Belize District	Cayo District	Stann Creek District	Toledo District	Ambergris Caye	other cayes
COLUMBIDAE (Pigeons and Doves)									(19)
Columba livia ROCK DOVE	AG	cP	cP	vP	cP	cP	cP	IP	IP
Columba cayennensis PALE-VENTED PIGEON	BFL,PFL,MF,AG sa	fP	cP	vP	cP	vP	vP	uV	uV
Columba speciosa SCALED PIGEON	BFM,BFL pfm,pfl	uP	fP	uP	fP	fP	uP		
Columba leucocephala WHITE-CROWNED PIGEON[56]	MF	X	X	rW		rW		cS	cS
Columba flavirostris RED-BILLED PIGEON[57]	BFL,PFL sc,ag	vP	vP	u?P	cP	rP	oV		
Columba nigrirostris SHORT-BILLED PIGEON	BFM,BFL		cP	fP	cP	cP	cP		
Streptopelia decaocto EURASIAN COLLARED-DOVE[58]	AG							X	
Zenaida asiatica WHITE-WINGED DOVE[59]	AG sc	cP	fT	fT	oT	oT	oT	cP	IP
Zenaida macroura MOURNING DOVE[60]	AG	uT	uT	uT	uT	uT	uT	uT	uT
Columbina inca INCA DOVE[61]	AG					X			
Columbina passerina COMMON GROUND-DOVE	SA,AG	cP	mP	fP	oV	mP	oV		IP
Columbina minuta PLAIN-BREASTED GROUND-DOVE	SA,AG sc	fP	cP	cP	uP	cP	cP		
Columbina talpacoti RUDDY GROUND-DOVE	SC,AG sa	vP	vP	vP	cP	vP	vP	?	
Claravis pretiosa BLUE GROUND-DOVE	BFM,BFL,PFM pfl,sc,ag	lP	cP	uP	cP	fP	cP		
Leptotila verreauxi WHITE-TIPPED DOVE	BFL,PFM,PFL,SC ag	cP	cP	cP	cP	cP	mP		
Leptotila rufaxilla GRAY-FRONTED DOVE	BFM,BFL	lP	cP	cP	cP	cP	cP		
Leptotila jamaicensis CARIBBEAN DOVE[62]	MF							cP	oV
Leptotila cassini GRAY-CHESTED DOVE	BFM,BFL			mP	lP	fP	cP		
Geotrygon montana RUDDY QUAIL-DOVE[63]	BFM,BFL ag	uP	fP	fP	fP	fP	fP		X

Forested Habitats: BFM/bfm = submontane broadleaf forest; BFL/bfl = lowland broadleaf forest; PFM/pfm = submontane pine forest; PFL/pfl = lowland pine forest; MF/mf = mangrove and littoral forest.
Transitional Habitats: SC/sc = scrub, low second growth; SA/sa = savanna.
Unforested Habitats: AG/ag = cultivated land, pastureland, ornamental vegetation; WL/wl = wetland habitats with emergent vegetation ; LA/la = lagoons, ponds, rivers, streams; BE/be = coastal habitats; OC/oc = ocean.

PSITTACIFORMES

PSITTACIDAE (Parrots) (10)

	Habitats	Corozal District	Orange Walk District	Belize District	Cayo District	Stann Creek District	Toledo District	Ambergris Caye	other cayes
Aratinga nana OLIVE-THROATED PARAKEET[64]	BFL,PFM,PFL,SC,AG bfm	cP	vP	vP	vP	vP	vP	cP	oW
Ara macao SCARLET MACAW	BFL pfm,pfl				IP	IV	oV		
Pionopsitta haematotis BROWN-HOODED PARROT	BFM,BFL sc			cP	uP	fP	cP	cP	
Pionus senilis WHITE-CROWNED PARROT	BFM,BFL sc	fP	cP	cP	cP	cP	cP		
Amazona albifrons WHITE-FRONTED PARROT	BFL,SA,AG	vP	vP	vP	vP	IP			
Amazona xantholora YELLOW-LORED PARROT	BFL,SA,AG	vP	IP	fP	mP	mP?			
Amazona autumnalis RED-LORED PARROT	BFL,PFM,PFL,AG sa	oP	vP	vP	vP	vP	vP		
Amazona farinosa MEALY PARROT	BFM,BFL pfm			fP	IP	cP	cP	cP	
Amazona oratrix YELLOW-HEADED PARROT	PFL,SA ag			fP	fP	mP	fP	fP	
Amazona auropalliata YELLOW-NAPED PARROT[65]	MF								X

CUCULIFORMES

CUCULIDAE (Cuckoos and Anis) (8)

	Habitats	Corozal District	Orange Walk District	Belize District	Cayo District	Stann Creek District	Toledo District	Ambergris Caye	other cayes
Coccyzus erythropthalmus BLACK-BILLED CUCKOO	BFM,BFL,MF sc		X	X			rT	rT	rT
Coccyzus americanus YELLOW-BILLED CUCKOO	BFM,BFL,MF pfm,pfl,sc	uT	oT	uT	oT	uT	uT	uT	fT
Coccyzus minor MANGROVE CUCKOO[66]	MF ag	rP?	rP?	X?	rP?	rP?	rP	IP	
Piaya cayana SQUIRREL CUCKOO	BFM,BFL,PFM,PFL	cP	cP	cP	cP	cP	cP	uP	
Tapera naevia STRIPED CUCKOO	SC	uP	uP	uP	uP	uP	uP		
Dromococcyx phasianellus PHEASANT CUCKOO	BFM,BFL,SC	?	rP	rP	rP	rP	rP		

Key simbols:

Abundance: v = very common; c = common; f = fairly common; u = uncommon; r = rare; o = occasional; l = uncommon or even common locally, but absent or scarce in most of the district; m = marginally occurs in district.

Seasonality: P = permanent resident; S = seasonal resident only; V = visitor; T = transient; W = winter resident; X = known from only one or two records.

Habitats	Corozal District	Orange Walk District	Belize District	Cayo District	Stann Creek District	Toledo District	Ambergris Caye	other cayes
Crotophaga ani SMOOTH-BILLED ANI[67]	MF,AG sc							oW	oT
Crotophaga sulcirostris GROOVE-BILLED ANI	SC,AG mf	vP	vP	vP	vP	vP	vP	cP	oW

STRIGIFORMES

TYTONIDAE (Barn Owls) (1)

Habitats	Corozal District	Orange Walk District	Belize District	Cayo District	Stann Creek District	Toledo District	Ambergris Caye	other cayes
Tyto alba BARN OWL	AG wl	uP	uP	uP	uP	uP	uP		

STRIGIDAE (Typical Owls) (12)

Habitats	Corozal District	Orange Walk District	Belize District	Cayo District	Stann Creek District	Toledo District	Ambergris Caye	other cayes
Otus guatemalae VERMICULATED SCREECH-OWL	BFM,BFL,PFM,PFL	uP	uP	uP	uP	uP	uP		
Lophostrix cristata CRESTED OWL	BFM,BFL				IP	IP	IP		
Pulsatrix perspicillata SPECTACLED OWL	BFM,BFL			rP	uP	uP	uP		
Bubo virginianus GREAT HORNED OWL	AG				rP?		X	uP	
Glaucidium griseiceps CENTRAL AMERICAN PYGMY-OWL	BFM,BFL			rP	IP	uP	uP		
Glaucidium brasilianum FERRUGINOUS PYGMY-OWL	PFM,PFL,AG bfm,bfl	fP	uP	I?P	fP	IP	IP		
Athene cunicularia BURROWING OWL[68]	AG				X		X		
Ciccaba virgata MOTTLED OWL	BFM,BFL,PFM,PFL	cP	cP	cP	cP	cP	cP	rP	
Ciccaba nigrolineata BLACK-AND-WHITE OWL	BFL			uP	uP	rP	rP		
Asio stygius STYGIAN OWL	PFM,PFL			rP	rP	rP	rP		
Asio flammeus SHORT-EARED OWL[69]	WL ag						X		
Pseudoscops clamator STRIPED OWL	SA,AG				mP		uP	uP	

Forested Habitats: BFM/bfm = submontane broadleaf forest; BFL/bfl = lowland broadleaf forest; PFM/pfm = submontane pine forest; PFL/pfl = lowland pine forest; MF/mf = mangrove and littoral forest.
Transitional Habitats: SC/sc = scrub, low second growth; SA/sa = savanna.
Unforested Habitats: AG/ag = cultivated land, pastureland, ornamental vegetation; WL/wl = wetland habitats with emergent vegetation ; LA/la = lagoons, ponds, rivers, streams; BE/be = coastal habitats; OC/oc = ocean.

25

Habitats	Corozal District	Orange Walk District	Belize District	Cayo District	Stann Creek District	Toledo District	Ambergris Caye	other cayes

CAPRIMULGIFORMES

CAPRIMULGIDAE (Nightjars) (8)

Species	Habitats	Corozal District	Orange Walk District	Belize District	Cayo District	Stann Creek District	Toledo District	Ambergris Caye	other cayes
Lurocalis semitorquatus SHORT-TAILED NIGHTHAWK[70]	LA mf					X			X
Chordeiles acutipennis LESSER NIGHTHAWK	SA,AG,WL	fW	uW	fW	uW	fW	fW	fT	uT
Chordeiles minor COMMON NIGHTHAWK	PFM,PFL,SA,AG	cT	IS	IS?	IS	IS?	IS	cT	uT
Nyctidromus albicollis COMMON PAURAQUE	BFM,BFL,PFM,PFL SC,SA,AG	cP	cP	cP	cP	cP	cP	cP	
Nyctiphrynus yucatanicus YUCATAN POORWILL	BFL,SC	u?P	uP	uP	IP				
Caprimulgus carolinensis CHUCK-WILL'S-WIDOW[71]	BFM,BFL,MF,SC,AG		oT		oT		oT		uT
Caprimulgus badius YUCATAN NIGHTJAR[72]	BFL	uW	uW	uW	uW		X	X	X
Caprimulgus vociferus WHIP-POOR-WILL[73]	BFM,BFL,SC				X	X	X	X	

NYCTIBIIDAE (Potoos) (1)

Species	Habitats	Corozal District	Orange Walk District	Belize District	Cayo District	Stann Creek District	Toledo District	Ambergris Caye	other cayes
Nyctibius jamaicensis NORTHERN POTOO	SA,AG	uP	uP	uP	uP	uP	uP	rP?	

APODIFORMES

APODIDAE (Swifts) (6)

Species	Habitats	Corozal District	Orange Walk District	Belize District	Cayo District	Stann Creek District	Toledo District	Ambergris Caye	other cayes
Cypseloides cryptus WHITE-CHINNED SWIFT[74]	Aerial				?	X			
Streptoprocne rutila CHESTNUT-COLLARED SWIFT[75]	Aerial				X	X			
Streptoprocne zonaris WHITE-COLLARED SWIFT	Aerial			uP	uP	cP	fP	fP	
Chaetura pelagica CHIMNEY SWIFT	Aerial	fT	?T	fT	?T	fT	fT	oT	oT
Chaetura vauxi VAUX'S SWIFT	Aerial	uP	fP	f?P	cP	cP	cP		
Panyptila cayennensis LESSER SWALLOW-TAILED SWIFT	Aerial			fP	uP	fP	fP	fP	

Key simbols:
Abundance: v = very common; c = common; f = fairly common; u = uncommon; r = rare; o = occasional; l = uncommon or even common locally, but absent or scarce in most of the district; m = marginally occurs in district.
Seasonality: P = permanent resident; S = seasonal resident only; V = visitor; T = transient; W = winter resident; X = known from only one or two records.

TROCHILIDAE (Hummingbirds)									**(22)**
Threnetes ruckeri BAND-TAILED BARBTHROAT	BFL sc					rP	lP		
Phaethornis superciliosus LONG-TAILED HERMIT	BFM,BFL,SC		lP	uP	cP	cP	cP		
Phaethornis longuemareus LITTLE HERMIT	BFM,BFL	uP	cP	fP	cP	cP	cP		
Phaeochroa cuvieri SCALY-BREASTED HUMMINGBIRD	BFM,BFL sc		uP	mP	uP	uP	uP		
Campylopterus curvipennis WEDGE-TAILED SABREWING	BFM,BFL,PFM,PFL sc	fP	fP	mP	fP	lP	lP		
Campylopterus hemileucurus VIOLET SABREWING	BFM bfl				fP	fP	fP		
Florisuga mellivora WHITE-NECKED JACOBIN	BFM,BFL,LA		uP	uP	fP	fP	fP		
Colibri delphinae BROWN VIOLET-EAR[76]	BFM	X	X			rP	lP		
Anthracothorax prevostii GREEN-BREASTED MANGO	MF,AG	uP	uP	uP	uP	uP	fP		cP
Lophornis helenae BLACK-CRESTED COQUETTE	BFM,BFL sc				rP	X	rP		
Chlorostilbon canivetii CANIVET'S EMERALD	PFM,PFL,SA,SC,AG	cP	fP	cP	fP	fP	lP	uP	X
Thalurania colombica VIOLET-CROWNED WOODNYMPH[77]	BFM bfl				X		lP		
Hylocharis eliciae BLUE-THROATED GOLDENTAIL[78]	SC,AG				X		X		
Amazilia candida WHITE-BELLIED EMERALD	BFM,BFL pfl	fP	cP	fP	cP	cP	cP		
Amazilia cyanocephala AZURE-CROWNED HUMMINGBIRD	PFM,PFL bfm		lP	cP	cP	cP	lP		
Amazilia tzacatl RUFOUS-TAILED HUMMINGBIRD	SC,SA,AG bfl,pfm,pfl	cP	vP	vP	vP	vP	vP	oV	X
Amazilia yucatanensis BUFF-BELLIED HUMMINGBIRD	SC,SA ag	fP	uP	fP	lP	lP			
Amazilia rutila CINNAMON HUMMINGBIRD	MF,AG	lP	mP	lP		lP	lP	●	cP
Eupherusa eximia STRIPE-TAILED HUMMINGBIRD	BFM				cP	cP	cP		

Forested Habitats: BFM/bfm = submontane broadleaf forest; BFL/bfl = lowland broadleaf forest; PFM/pfm = submontane pine forest; PFL/pfl = lowland pine forest; MF/mf = mangrove and littoral forest.
Transitional Habitats: SC/sc = scrub, low second growth; SA/sa = savanna.
Unforested Habitats: AG/ag = cultivated land, pastureland, ornamental vegetation; WL/wl = wetland habitats with emergent vegetation ; LA/la = lagoons, ponds, rivers, streams; BE/be = coastal habitats; OC/oc = ocean.

	Habitats	Corozal District	Orange Walk District	Belize District	Cayo District	Stann Creek District	Toledo District	Ambergris Caye	other cayes
Heliothryx barroti PURPLE-CROWNED FAIRY[79]	BFM,BFL		uP	mP?	uP	uP	uP		X
Heliomaster longirostris LONG-BILLED STARTHROAT[80]	SC,AG			X	X		X		
Archilochus colubris RUBY-THROATED HUMMINGBIRD	SC,AG	uW	uW	uW	uW	uW	uW	uW	uT

TROGONIFORMES

TROGONIDAE (Trogons) (4)

	Habitats	Corozal District	Orange Walk District	Belize District	Cayo District	Stann Creek District	Toledo District	Ambergris Caye	other cayes
Trogon melanocephalus BLACK-HEADED TROGON[81]	BFL,PFM,PFL,AG	cP	cP	cP	cP	cP	cP	uP	oW
Trogon violaceus VIOLACEOUS TROGON	BFM,BFL,PFM,PFL ag	cP	cP	cP	cP	cP	cP		
Trogon collaris COLLARED TROGON	BFM,BFL			lP	fP	fP	fP		
Trogon massena SLATY-TAILED TROGON	BFM,BFL pfm		cP	mP?	cP	cP	cP		

CORACIIFORMES

MOMOTIDAE (Motmots) (3)

	Habitats	Corozal District	Orange Walk District	Belize District	Cayo District	Stann Creek District	Toledo District	Ambergris Caye	other cayes
Hylomanes momotula TODY MOTMOT	BFM,BFL pfm		fP	?P	fP	fP	fP		
Momotus momota BLUE-CROWNED MOTMOT	BFM,BFL,PFM,PFL	cP	cP	cP	cP	cP	cP		
Electron carinatum KEEL-BILLED MOTMOT	BFM,BFL				uP	uP	uP		

ALCEDINIDAE (Kingfishers) (5)

	Habitats	Corozal District	Orange Walk District	Belize District	Cayo District	Stann Creek District	Toledo District	Ambergris Caye	other cayes
Ceryle torquata RINGED KINGFISHER	LA	fP	fP	cP	fP	fP	fP	oV	
Ceryle alcyon BELTED KINGFISHER	LA,BE wl	cW	fW	cW	fW	cW	cW		cW
Chloroceryle amazona AMAZON KINGFISHER	LA	?	uP	uP	uP	uP	uP		
Chloroceryle americana GREEN KINGFISHER[82]	LA wl	fP	fP	cP	cP	cP	cP	X	

Key simbols:
Abundance: v = very common; c = common; f = fairly common; u = uncommon; r = rare; o = occasional; l = uncommon or even common locally, but absent or scarce in most of the district; m = marginally occurs in district.
Seasonality: P = permanent resident; S = seasonal resident only; V = visitor; T = transient; W = winter resident; X = known from only one or two records.

Habitats	Corozal District	Orange Walk District	Belize District	Cayo District	Stann Creek District	Toledo District	Ambergris Caye	other cayes
Chloroceryle aenea AMERICAN PYGMY KINGFISHER[83] LA wl	IP	IP	cP	IP	cP	cP		X

PICIFORMES

BUCCONIDAE (Puffbirds) (2)

	Corozal District	Orange Walk District	Belize District	Cayo District	Stann Creek District	Toledo District	Ambergris Caye	other cayes
Notharchus macrorhynchos WHITE-NECKED PUFFBIRD SC,AG bfl	uP	uP	uP	rP	rP	rP		
Malacoptila panamensis WHITE-WHISKERED PUFFBIRD BFM,BFL pfm,pfl		uP	mP	uP	uP	uP		

GALBULIDAE (Jacamars) (1)

	Corozal District	Orange Walk District	Belize District	Cayo District	Stann Creek District	Toledo District	Ambergris Caye	other cayes
Galbula ruficauda RUFOUS-TAILED JACAMAR BFM,BFL sc		fP	uP	fP	fP	fP		

RAMPHASTIDAE (Toucans) (3)

	Corozal District	Orange Walk District	Belize District	Cayo District	Stann Creek District	Toledo District	Ambergris Caye	other cayes
Aulacorhynchus prasinus EMERALD TOUCANET BFM,PFM bfl		IP	oV	fP	fP	fP		
Pteroglossus torquatus COLLARED ARACARI BFM,BFL pfm,pfl	cP	cP	cP	cP	cP	cP	rP?	
Ramphastos sulfuratus KEEL-BILLED TOUCAN BFM,BFL,PFM,PFL	fP	cP	fP	cP	cP	cP		

PICIDAE (Woodpeckers) (11)

	Corozal District	Orange Walk District	Belize District	Cayo District	Stann Creek District	Toledo District	Ambergris Caye	other cayes
Melanerpes formicivorus ACORN WOODPECKER PFM,PFL		cP	cP	cP	cP	cP		
Melanerpes pucherani BLACK-CHEEKED WOODPECKER BFM,BFL		fP	IP	fP	fP	fP		
Melanerpes pygmaeus RED-VENTED WOODPECKER PFL,MF,AG bfl	cP	IP	fP	mP?			uP	IP
Melanerpes aurifrons GOLDEN-FRONTED WOODPECKER SC,AG	cP	cP	cP	cP	cP	cP	*cP*	IP
Sphyrapicus varius YELLOW-BELLIED SAPSUCKER BFM,BFL,PFM,PFL MF,AG	uW	uW	uW	uW	uW	uW	uW	uT
Picoides scalaris LADDER-BACKED WOODPECKER PFL		mP	fP	mP	fP	fP		

Red Bellied Wood Pecker (handwritten)

Forested Habitats: BFM/bfm = submontane broadleaf forest; BFL/bfl = lowland broadleaf forest; PFM/pfm = submontane pine forest; PFL/pfl = lowland pine forest; MF/mf = mangrove and littoral forest.
Transitional Habitats: SC/sc = scrub, low second growth; SA/sa = savanna.
Unforested Habitats: AG/ag = cultivated land, pastureland, ornamental vegetation; WL/wl = wetland habitats with emergent vegetation ; LA/la = lagoons, ponds, rivers, streams; BE/be = coastal habitats; OC/oc = ocean.

	Habitats	Corozal District	Orange Walk District	Belize District	Cayo District	Stann Creek District	Toledo District	Ambergris Caye	other cayes
Veniliornis fumigatus SMOKY-BROWN WOODPECKER	BFM,BFL	uP	fP	fP	fP	fP	fP		
Piculus rubiginosus GOLDEN-OLIVE WOODPECKER	BFM,BFL,PFM,PFL	fP	fP	fP	cP	fP	fP		
Celeus castaneus CHESTNUT-COLORED WOODPECKER	BFM,BFL	uP	fP	uP	uP	uP	uP		
Dryocopus lineatus LINEATED WOODPECKER	BFM,BFL,PFM,PFL AG	cP	cP	cP	cP	cP	cP	uP	
Campephilus guatemalensis PALE-BILLED WOODPECKER	BFM,BFL,PFM,PFL ag	fP	cP	cP	cP	cP	cP		

PASSERIFORMES

FURNARIIDAE (Ovenbirds) (6)

	Habitats	Corozal District	Orange Walk District	Belize District	Cayo District	Stann Creek District	Toledo District	Ambergris Caye	other cayes
Synallaxis erythrothorax RUFOUS-BREASTED SPINETAIL	SC	uP	fP	fP	fP	fP	fP		
Anabacerthia variegaticeps SCALY-THROATED FOLIAGE-GLEANER[84]	BFM				IP		IP		
Automolus ochrolaemus BUFF-THROATED FOLIAGE-GLEANER	BFM,BFL		uP	mP?	fP	fP	fP		
Xenops minutus PLAIN XENOPS	BFM,BFL pfm,pfl	fP	cP	fP	cP	cP	cP		
Sclerurus mexicanus TAWNY-THROATED LEAFTOSSER[85]	BFM				IP		IP		
Sclerurus guatemalensis SCALY-THROATED LEAFTOSSER	BFM,BFL		uP		uP	uP	uP		

DENDROCOLAPTIDAE (Woodcreepers) (9)

	Habitats	Corozal District	Orange Walk District	Belize District	Cayo District	Stann Creek District	Toledo District	Ambergris Caye	other cayes
Dendrocincla anabatina TAWNY-WINGED WOODCREEPER	BFM,BFL	uP	fP	fP	fP	fP	fP		
Dendrocincla homochroa RUDDY WOODCREEPER	BFM,BFL	uP	fP	uP	uP	uP	uP		
Sittasomus griseicapillus OLIVACEOUS WOODCREEPER	BFM,BFL,PFM,PFL	uP	fP	fP	fP	fP	fP		
Glyphorynchus spirurus WEDGE-BILLED WOODCREEPER	BFM,BFL		IP	IP	fP	fP	fP		
Xiphocolaptes promeropirhynchus STRONG-BILLED WOODCREEPER	BFM,BFL		IP		IP		IP		

Key simbols:
Abundance: v = very common; c = common; f = fairly common; u = uncommon; r = rare; o = occasional; l = uncommon or even common locally, but absent or scarce in most of the district; m = marginally occurs in district.
Seasonality: P = permanent resident; S = seasonal resident only; V = visitor; T = transient; W = winter resident; X = known from only one or two records.

Habitats	Corozal District	Orange Walk District	Belize District	Cayo District	Stann Creek District	Toledo District	Ambergris Caye	other caves
Dendrocolaptes sanctithomae NORTHERN BARRED-WOODCREEPER · BFM,BFL,PFL	fP	fP	fP	fP	fP	fP		
Xiphorhynchus flavigaster IVORY-BILLED WOODCREEPER · BFM,BFL ag	fP	cP	cP	cP	cP	cP		
Xiphorhynchus erythropygius SPOTTED WOODCREEPER · BFM				fP	?	fP		
Lepidocolaptes souleyetii STREAK-HEADED WOODCREEPER · BFM,BFL,PFM,PFL	?	uP	uP	uP	uP	uP		

THAMNOPHILIDAE (Antbirds) (9)

Habitats	Corozal District	Orange Walk District	Belize District	Cayo District	Stann Creek District	Toledo District	Ambergris Caye	other caves
Taraba major GREAT ANTSHRIKE · SC bfl		mP	lP	uP	uP	fP		
Thamnophilus doliatus BARRED ANTSHRIKE · SC bfl	fP	cP	cP	cP	cP	cP		
Thamnophilus atrinucha WESTERN SLATY-ANTSHRIKE · BFL						fP		
Thamnistes anabatinus RUSSET ANTSHRIKE · BFM bfl					lP	uP		
Dysithamnus mentalis PLAIN ANTVIREO · BFM,BFL			lP	lP	lP	lP		
Myrmotherula schisticolor SLATY ANTWREN[86] · BFM				fP		fP		
Microrhopias quixensis DOT-WINGED ANTWREN · BFL bfm,pfm		cP	cP	cP	cP	cP		
Cercomacra tyrannina DUSKY ANTBIRD · SC		fP	fP	cP	cP	cP		
Gymnocichla nudiceps BARE-CROWNED ANTBIRD · SC				rP	rP	lP		

FORMICARIIDAE (Antthrushes) (1)

Habitats	Corozal District	Orange Walk District	Belize District	Cayo District	Stann Creek District	Toledo District	Ambergris Caye	other caves
Formicarius analis BLACK-FACED ANTTHRUSH · BFM,BFL	fP	cP	cP	cP	cP	cP		

TYRANNIDAE (Tyrant Flycatchers) (49)

Habitats	Corozal District	Orange Walk District	Belize District	Cayo District	Stann Creek District	Toledo District	Ambergris Caye	other caves
Ornithion semiflavum YELLOW-BELLIED TYRANNULET · BFM,BFL		fP	lP	fP	fP	fP		
Camptostoma imberbe NORTHERN BEARDLESS-TYRANNULET · PFL,SC,SA,AG	fP	fP	fP	lP	fP	lP		

Forested Habitats: BFM/bfm = submontane broadleaf forest; BFL/bfl = lowland broadleaf forest; PFM/pfm = submontane pine forest; PFL/pfl = lowland pine forest; MF/mf = mangrove and littoral forest.
Transitional Habitats: SC/sc = scrub, low second growth; SA/sa = savanna.
Unforested Habitats: AG/ag = cultivated land, pastureland, ornamental vegetation; WL/wl = wetland habitats with emergent vegetation ; LA/la = lagoons, ponds, rivers, streams; BE/be = coastal habitats; OC/oc = ocean.

31

Habitats	Corozal District	Orange Walk District	Belize District	Cayo District	Stann Creek District	Toledo District	Ambergris Caye	other cayes
Myiopagis viridicata GREENISH ELAENIA — BFM,BFL,AG	fP	fP	fP	fP	fP	fP	X	
Elaenia martinica CARIBBEAN ELAENIA[87] — MF			X				uW	IP
Elaenia flavogaster YELLOW-BELLIED ELAENIA[88] — PFM,PFL,SA,AG sc	cP	cP	vP	vP	vP	vP	cP	oT
Mionectes oleagineus OCHRE-BELLIED FLYCATCHER — BFM,BFL,PFM	fP	cP	fP	cP	cP	cP		
Leptopogon amaurocephalus SEPIA-CAPPED FLYCATCHER — BFM,BFL	?	uP	IP	fP	fP	fP		
Zimmerius vilissimus PALTRY TYRANNULET[89] — BFL,AG						IP		
Oncostoma cinereigulare NORTHERN BENTBILL — BFM,BFL,PFM sc	cP	cP	cP	cP	cP	cP		
Poecilotriccus sylvia SLATE-HEADED TODY-FLYCATCHER — SC		uP	uP	uP	uP	uP		
Todirostrum cinereum COMMON TODY-FLYCATCHER — SC,SA,AG	uP	cP	cP	cP	cP	cP	cP	
Rhynchocyclus brevirostris EYE-RINGED FLATBILL — BFM,BFL	uP	uP	uP	uP	uP	uP		
Tolmomyias sulphurescens YELLOW-OLIVE FLYCATCHER — BFM,BFL,PFM,PFL ag	cP	cP	cP	cP	cP	cP		
Platyrinchus cancrominus STUB-TAILED SPADEBILL — BFM,BFL	fP	cP	fP	cP	cP	cP		
Onychorhynchus coronatus ROYAL FLYCATCHER — BFM,BFL	uP	uP	uP	uP	uP	uP		
Terenotriccus erythrurus RUDDY-TAILED FLYCATCHER — BFM,BFL		uP		rP	rP	rP		
Myiobius sulphureipygius SULPHUR-RUMPED FLYCATCHER — BFM,BFL		cP	IP	cP	cP	cP		
Contopus cooperi OLIVE-SIDED FLYCATCHER[90] — BFM,BFL,PFM,PFL AG	uT	uT	uT	uT	uT	uT	uT	uT
Contopus pertinax GREATER PEWEE — PFM					fP			
Contopus sordidulus WESTERN WOOD-PEWEE[91] — PFM					X			
Contopus virens EASTERN WOOD-PEWEE — BFM,BFL,PFM,PFL SC,AG	vT	vT	vT	vT	vT	vT	vT	vT
Contopus cinereus TROPICAL PEWEE — BFM,BFL,PFM,PFL sc,ag	uP	fP	fP	fP	fP	fP		

Key simbols:

Abundance: v = very common; c = common; f = fairly common; u = uncommon; r = rare; o = occasional; l = uncommon or even common locally, but absent or scarce in most of the district; m = marginally occurs in district.

Seasonality: P = permanent resident; S = seasonal resident only; V = visitor; T = transient; W = winter resident; X = known from only one or two records.

Habitats	Corozal District	Orange Walk District	Belize District	Cayo District	Stann Creek District	Toledo District	Ambergris Caye	other cayes
Empidonax flaviventris YELLOW-BELLIED FLYCATCHER BFM,BFL,PFM pfl	fW	fW	fW	cW	cW	cW	uW	cT
Empidonax virescens ACADIAN FLYCATCHER SC,AG	uT	uT	uT	uT	uT	uT	fT	cT
Empidonax alnorum ALDER FLYCATCHER[92] SC,AG	?	?	?	?	?	uT	uT	uT
Empidonax traillii WILLOW FLYCATCHER[93] SC,AG	?	?	?	?	uT	fT	fT	fT
Empidonax albigularis WHITE-THROATED FLYCATCHER[94] WL			IW	IW	IW	X		
Empidonax minimus LEAST FLYCATCHER SC,AG	cW	cW	cW	cW	cW	cW	cW	fW
Sayornis nigricans BLACK PHOEBE LA		mP	IP	IP	IP	IP		
Pyrocephalus rubinus VERMILION FLYCATCHER SA,AG	fP	cP	cP	fP	cP	mP	oV	X
Attila spadiceus BRIGHT-RUMPED ATTILA BFM,BFL,PFM,PFL	cP	cP	IP	cP	cP	cP		
Rhytipterna holerythra RUFOUS MOURNER BFM,BFL		uP		uP	uP	uP		
Myiarchus yucatanensis YUCATAN FLYCATCHER BFL,SC	fP	uP	uP				rP	
Myiarchus tuberculifer DUSKY-CAPPED FLYCATCHER BFM,BFL,PFM,PFL ag,sc	cP	cP	cP	cP	cP	cP	cP	IP?
Myiarchus crinitus GREAT CRESTED FLYCATCHER BFM,BFL,PFM,PFL ag	fW	fW	fW	fW	fW	fW	cT	cT
Myiarchus tyrannulus BROWN-CRESTED FLYCATCHER[95] BFL,PFM,PFL,AG	cS	cS	cS	cS	cS	cS	uS	oT
Pitangus sulphuratus GREAT KISKADEE[96] SC,AG sa,wl	vP	vP	vP	vP	vP	vP	vP	IW
Megarynchus pitangua BOAT-BILLED FLYCATCHER BFM,BFL pfm,pfl,ag	cP	cP	cP	cP	cP	cP		
Myiozetetes similis SOCIAL FLYCATCHER SC,AG bfl,pfm,pfl	vP	vP	vP	vP	vP	vP		
Myiodynastes maculatus STREAKED FLYCATCHER BFM,BFL	?	uS	?	uS	IS	IS		
Myiodynastes luteiventris SULPHUR-BELLIED FLYCATCHER BFM,BFL pfm	cS	cS	cS	cS	cS	cS		oT
Legatus leucophaius PIRATIC FLYCATCHER BFL,AG	IS	fS	fS	fS	fS	fS		

Forested Habitats: BFM/bfm = submontane broadleaf forest; BFL/bfl = lowland broadleaf forest; PFM/pfm = submontane pine forest; PFL/pfl = lowland pine forest; MF/mf = mangrove and littoral forest.
Transitional Habitats: SC/sc = scrub, low second growth; SA/sa = savanna.
Unforested Habitats: AG/ag = cultivated land, pastureland, ornamental vegetation; WL/wl = wetland habitats with emergent vegetation ; LA/la = lagoons, ponds, rivers, streams; BE/be = coastal habitats; OC/oc = ocean.

	Habitats	Corozal District	Orange Walk District	Belize District	Cayo District	Stann Creek District	Toledo District	Ambergris Caye	other cayes
Tyrannus melancholicus TROPICAL KINGBIRD	PFM,PFL,SA,SC,AG	vP	vP	vP	vP	vP	vP	vP	IP
Tyrannus couchii COUCH'S KINGBIRD	PFM,PFL,SA,SC,AG	cP	cP	cP	cP	cP	cP	fP	IP
Tyrannus vociferans CASSIN'S KINGBIRD[97]	AG		X						
Tyrannus tyrannus EASTERN KINGBIRD	BFL,AG sc	vT	cT	vT	cT	vT	vT	vT	cT
Tyrannus dominicensis GRAY KINGBIRD[98]	MF,AG sc		X	oW	X	X		oW	oT
Tyrannus forficatus SCISSOR-TAILED FLYCATCHER[99]	AG sa		IW	uW	o?W	uW	uW	oT	oT
Tyrannus savanna FORK-TAILED FLYCATCHER	SA,AG		cP	cP	cP	cP	IP		

Genera INCERTAE SEDIS (species of uncertain affinities) (9)

	Habitats	Corozal District	Orange Walk District	Belize District	Cayo District	Stann Creek District	Toledo District	Ambergris Caye	other cayes
Schiffornis turdinus THRUSH-LIKE SCHIFFORNIS	BFM,BFL,PFM	fP	cP	cP	cP	cP	cP		
Lipaugus unirufus RUFOUS PIHA	BFM,BFL		IP	IP	uP	uP	uP		
Laniocera rufescens SPECKLED MOURNER	BFM,BFL			rP		rP	rP	rP	
Pachyramphus cinnamomeus CINNAMON BECARD	BFM,BFL		IP	IP	fP	fP	fP		
Pachyramphus polychopterus WHITE-WINGED BECARD[100]	SC,AG		IP	IP	IP	IP	IP		
Pachyramphus major GRAY-COLLARED BECARD	BFL			rP	rP	rP	rP	rP	
Pachyramphus aglaiae ROSE-THROATED BECARD	BFL,PFM,PFL,AG	cP	fP	fP	fP	uP	uP	rP?	
Tityra semifasciata MASKED TITYRA	BFM,BFL,PFM,PFL ag	cP	cP	cP	cP	cP	cP	rP?	
Tityra inquisitor BLACK-CROWNED TITYRA	BFL	IP	fP	fP	fP	fP	fP		

COTINGIDAE (Cotingas) (1)

	Habitats	Corozal District	Orange Walk District	Belize District	Cayo District	Stann Creek District	Toledo District	Ambergris Caye	other cayes
Cotinga amabilis LOVELY COTINGA	BFM,BFL			rP		rP	rP	rP	

Key simbols:
Abundance: v = very common; c = common; f = fairly common; u = uncommon; r = rare; o = occasional; l = uncommon or even common locally, but absent or scarce in most of the district; m = marginally occurs in district.
Seasonality: P = permanent resident; S = seasonal resident only; V = visitor; T = transient; W = winter resident; X = known from only one or two records.

Habitats	Corozal District	Orange Walk District	Belize District	Cayo District	Stann Creek District	Toledo District	Ambergris Caye	other cayes
PIPRIDAE (Manakins)								(2)
Manacus candei WHITE-COLLARED MANAKIN BFL pfm,pfl,ag,sc	?	cP	cP	cP	cP	cP		
Pipra mentalis RED-CAPPED MANAKIN BFM,BFL,PFM pfl	cP	cP	fP	cP	cP	cP		
VIREONIDAE (Vireos)								(15)
Vireo griseus WHITE-EYED VIREO MF,SC,AG bfm,bfl,pfl	cW	cW	cW	cW	cW	cW	cW	cT
Vireo pallens MANGROVE VIREO MF,SC ag,bfl,pfl	cP	cP	cP	fP	cP	cP	✔	IP
Vireo flavifrons YELLOW-THROATED VIREO BFM,BFL pfm,pfl	fW	fW	fW	fW	fW	fW	uW	fT
Vireo plumbeus PLUMBEOUS VIREO[101] BFM,PFM pfl				cP	rP	IP		
Vireo solitarius BLUE-HEADED VIREO[102] AG				X				
Vireo gilvus WARBLING VIREO[103] BFM,BFL,AG	?	X			X			
Vireo philadelphicus PHILADELPHIA VIREO BFL,AG bfm,sc	uW	uW	uW	uW	uW	uW	✔	fT
Vireo olivaceus RED-EYED VIREO BFM,BFL,PFM,PFL AG	vT	vT	vT	vT	vT	vT	vT	vT
Vireo flavoviridis YELLOW-GREEN VIREO BFM,BFL ag	cS	cS	cS	cS	cS	cS	fS	oT
Vireo altiloquus BLACK-WHISKERED VIREO[104] MF								X
Vireo magister YUCATAN VIREO MF	IP		IP		IP	IP	✊	vP
Hylophilus ochraceiceps TAWNY-CROWNED GREENLET BFM,BFL		cP	cP	cP	cP	cP		
Hylophilus decurtatus LESSER GREENLET BFM,BFL pfm,pfl	vP	vP	vP	vP	vP	vP		
Vireolanius pulchellus GREEN SHRIKE-VIREO BFM,BFL		cP	mP	cP	cP	cP		
Cyclarhis gujanensis RUFOUS-BROWED PEPPERSHRIKE SA,SC,AG	cP	cP	cP	mP	uP	IP		

Forested Habitats: BFM/bfm = submontane broadleaf forest; BFL/bfl = lowland broadleaf forest; PFM/pfm = submontane pine forest; PFL/pfl = lowland pine forest; MF/mf = mangrove and littoral forest.
Transitional Habitats: SC/sc = scrub, low second growth; SA/sa = savanna.
Unforested Habitats: AG/ag = cultivated land, pastureland, ornamental vegetation; WL/wl = wetland habitats with emergent vegetation ; LA/la = lagoons, ponds, rivers, streams; BE/be = coastal habitats; OC/oc = ocean.

Habitats	Corozal District	Orange Walk District	Belize District	Cayo District	Stann Creek District	Toledo District	Ambergris Caye	other cayes
CORVIDAE (Jays)								(3)
Cyanocorax yncas GREEN JAY — BFL,PFM,PFL	fP	fP	fP	cP	uP	uP		
Cyanocorax morio BROWN JAY — BFL,PFM,PFL ag	vP	vP	vP	vP	vP	vP		
Cyanocorax yucatanicus YUCATAN JAY — BFL,PFL	vP	lP	lP	mP	mP		uP	
HIRUNDINIDAE (Swallows)								(10)
Progne subis PURPLE MARTIN — AG la	vT	cT	vT	cT	vT	vT	vT	cT
Progne dominicensis SNOWY-BELLIED MARTIN[105] — AG				X				
Progne chalybea GRAY-BREASTED MARTIN[106] — AG	cS	cS	cS	cS	cS	cS	cT	uT
Tachycineta bicolor TREE SWALLOW — WL,LA ag	fW	fW	vW	fW	uW	uW	cW	uW
Tachycineta albilinea MANGROVE SWALLOW — LA ag,wl	cP	cP	cP	cP	cP	cP	🐦	lP
Stelgidopteryx serripennis NO. ROUGH-WINGED SWALLOW[107] — BFM,BFL,PFM,PFL SA,AG,WL,LA	cW	cW	cW	cW	cW	cW	cW	cT
Riparia riparia BANK SWALLOW — AG,WL,LA	cT	fT	cT	fT	cT	cT	uT	uT
Petrochelidon pyrrhonota CLIFF SWALLOW — AG,WL,LA	cT	fT	cT	fT	cT	cT	uT	uT
Petrochelidon fulva CAVE SWALLOW[108] — AG,WL,LA		X	X			X	X	X
Hirundo rustica BARN SWALLOW — SA,AG,WL,LA	vT	vT	vT	vT	vT	vT	cT	cT
TROGLODYTIDAE (Wrens)								(9)
Campylorhynchus zonatus BAND-BACKED WREN — BFM,BFL pfm		rP	rP	fP	lP	lP		
Thryothorus maculipectus SPOT-BREASTED WREN — BFM,BFL,PFM,PFL sc,ag	vP	vP	vP	vP	vP	vP		
Thryothorus ludovicianus CAROLINA WREN[109] — BFL		rP		rP				

Key simbols:

Abundance: v = very common; c = common; f = fairly common; u = uncommon; r = rare; o = occasional; l = uncommon or even common locally, but absent or scarce in most of the district; m = marginally occurs in district.

Seasonality: P = permanent resident; S = seasonal resident only; V = visitor; T = transient; W = winter resident; X = known from only one or two records.

Habitats	Corozal District	Orange Walk District	Belize District	Cayo District	Stann Creek District	Toledo District	Ambergris Caye	other cayes
Thryothorus modestus PLAIN WREN PFM bfl				IP				
Troglodytes aedon HOUSE WREN SC,AG sa	fP	fP	fP	fP	fP	fP		
Cistothorus platensis SEDGE WREN[110] SA				IP	IP	fP		
Uropsila leucogastra WHITE-BELLIED WREN BFL,PFM,PFL	cP	fP	fP	fP	mP?			
Henicorhina leucosticta WHITE-BREASTED WOOD-WREN BFM,BFL pfm,pfl	uP	cP	cP	cP	cP	cP		
Microcerculus philomela NIGHTINGALE WREN BFM,BFL				IP	IP	IP		

SYLVIIDAE (Gnatwrens and Gnatcatchers) (3)

Habitats	Corozal District	Orange Walk District	Belize District	Cayo District	Stann Creek District	Toledo District	Ambergris Caye	other cayes
Ramphocaenus melanurus LONG-BILLED GNATWREN BFM,BFL pfm,pfl,sc	fP	cP	fP	cP	cP	cP		
Polioptila caerulea BLUE-GRAY GNATCATCHER[111] PFM,PFL sc,ag	IP	cP	cP	cP	cP	cP	oT	oT
Polioptila plumbea TROPICAL GNATCATCHER BFM,BFL pfm,pfl	rP	fP	uP	fP	fP	fP		

TURDIDAE (Thrushes) (9)

Habitats	Corozal District	Orange Walk District	Belize District	Cayo District	Stann Creek District	Toledo District	Ambergris Caye	other cayes
Sialia sialis EASTERN BLUEBIRD PFM				IP				
Myadestes unicolor SLATE-COLORED SOLITAIRE BFM				cP	cP	cP		
Catharus fuscescens VEERY BFM,BFL	uT	uT	uT	uT	uT	uT	fT	fT
Catharus minimus GRAY-CHEEKED THRUSH BFM,BFL	uT	uT	uT	uT	uT	uT	uT	uT
Catharus ustulatus SWAINSON'S THRUSH BFM,BFL pfm,pfl	fT	fT	fT	fT	fT	fT	cT	cT
Hylocichla mustelina WOOD THRUSH BFM,BFL pfm,pfl	fW	cW	cW	cW	cW	cW	cW	cT
Turdus grayi CLAY-COLORED ROBIN BFL,SC,AG	cP	cP	cP	cP	cP	cP	oV	
Turdus assimilis WHITE-THROATED ROBIN BFM bfl			uP	cP	cP	cP		

Forested Habitats: BFM/bfm = submontane broadleaf forest; BFL/bfl = lowland broadleaf forest; PFM/pfm = submontane pine forest; PFL/pfl = lowland pine forest; MF/mf = mangrove and littoral forest.

Transitional Habitats: SC/sc = scrub, low second growth; SA/sa = savanna.

Unforested Habitats: AG/ag = cultivated land, pastureland, ornamental vegetation; WL/wl = wetland habitats with emergent vegetation ; LA/la = lagoons, ponds, rivers, streams; BE/be = coastal habitats; OC/oc = ocean.

	Habitats	Corozal District	Orange Walk District	Belize District	Cayo District	Stann Creek District	Toledo District	Ambergris Caye	other cayes
Turdus migratorius AMERICAN ROBIN[112]	AG		X						

MIMIDAE (Mockingbirds) (3)

	Habitats	Corozal District	Orange Walk District	Belize District	Cayo District	Stann Creek District	Toledo District	Ambergris Caye	other cayes
Dumetella carolinensis GRAY CATBIRD	BFM,BFL,PFM,PFL sc,ag	cW	cW	cW	cW	cW	cW	cW	vT
Melanoptila glabrirostris BLACK CATBIRD	MF bfl	IP	IP	IP			X	cP	IP
Mimus gilvus TROPICAL MOCKINGBIRD	SA,AG	vP	cP	vP	cP	cP	IP	cP	uP

BOMBYCILLIDAE (Waxwings) (1)

	Habitats	Corozal District	Orange Walk District	Belize District	Cayo District	Stann Creek District	Toledo District	Ambergris Caye	other cayes
Bombycilla cedrorum CEDAR WAXWING	AG	oW	oW	oW	oW	oW	oW	oT	oT

PARULIDAE (Wood Warblers) (43)

	Habitats	Corozal District	Orange Walk District	Belize District	Cayo District	Stann Creek District	Toledo District	Ambergris Caye	other cayes
Vermivora pinus BLUE-WINGED WARBLER	BFM,BFL,SC,AG pfm,pfl	fW	fW	fW	fW	fW	fW	uT	uT
Vermivora chrysoptera GOLDEN-WINGED WARBLER	BFM,BFL,SC,AG pfm,pfl	uT	oW	uT	uW	uW	uW	oT	oT
Vermivora peregrina TENNESSEE WARBLER	BFM,BFL,SC,AG pfm,pfl	cT	uW	fW	fW	fW	fW	cT	cT
Vermivora ruficapilla NASHVILLE WARBLER[113]	SC,AG		X	X	X		X		rT
Vermivora virginiae VIRGINIA'S WARBLER[114]	SC,AG		X	X		X			X
Parula americana NORTHERN PARULA	MF,PFL,AG bfl	cW	uW	fW	uW	uW	oW		cW
Parula pitiayumi TROPICAL PARULA[115]	BFM bfl				IP		IP		
Dendroica petechia YELLOW WARBLER[116]	MF,SC,AG	cW	cW	cW	cW	cW	cW	cW	cW
Dendroica pensylvanica CHESTNUT-SIDED WARBLER	BFM,BFL,SC,AG pfm,pfl	cT	fW	uW	uW	fW	cW	cT	cT
Dendroica magnolia MAGNOLIA WARBLER	BFM,BFL,PFM,PFL SC,AG	cW	cW	cW	cW	cW	cW	cW	cT
Dendroica tigrina CAPE MAY WARBLER	MF,AG		X	rW	X		X		uT

Key simbols:
Abundance: v = very common; c = common; f = fairly common; u = uncommon; r = rare; o = occasional; l = uncommon or even common locally, but absent or scarce in most of the district; m = marginally occurs in district.
Seasonality: P = permanent resident; S = seasonal resident only; V = visitor; T = transient; W = winter resident; X = known from only one or two records.

Habitats	Corozal District	Orange Walk District	Belize District	Cayo District	Stann Creek District	Toledo District	Ambergris Caye	other cayes
Dendroica caerulescens BLACK-THROATED BLUE WARBLER MF,AG bfl	?	oW	oW	oW	?	X	uW	uT
Dendroica coronata YELLOW-RUMPED WARBLER[117] PFL,SA,AG bfl,sc	uW	fW	fW	fW	uW	oW	uW	uT
Dendroica nigrescens BLACK-THROATED GRAY WARBLER[118] PFL,AG sc						X		
Dendroica virens BLACK-THROATED GREEN WARBLER BFM,BFL,PFM,PFL ag	fW	fW	fW	cW	fW	fW	uW	uW
Dendroica occidentalis HERMIT WARBLER[119] PFM,PFL,AG bfm,bfl,sc			X	X				
Dendroica fusca BLACKBURNIAN WARBLER BFM,BFL,AG pfm,pfl	fT	uT	fT	uT	fT	fT	fT	fT
Dendroica dominica YELLOW-THROATED WARBLER PFM,PFL,AG bfm,bfl	cW	cW	cW	cW	cW	cW	cW	cW
Dendroica graciae GRACE'S WARBLER PFM,PFL		cP	cP	cP	cP	cP		
Dendroica discolor PRAIRIE WARBLER SC,AG	?	X	oW		?	oT	cW	uW
Dendroica palmarum PALM WARBLER PFL,SA,AG	fW	oW	fW	oW	uW	oT	cW	cW
Dendroica castanea BAY-BREASTED WARBLER BFM,BFL pfm,pfl,ag	uT	uT	uT	uT	uT	uT	fT	fT
Dendroica striata BLACKPOLL WARBLER[120] MF,AG bfl		X						oT
Dendroica cerulea CERULEAN WARBLER[121] BFM,BFL ag	uT	uT	uT	uT	uT	uT	oT	oT
Mniotilta varia BLACK-AND-WHITE WARBLER BFM,BFL,PFM,PFL AG	cW	cW	cW	cW	cW	cW	cW	cW
Setophaga ruticilla AMERICAN REDSTART BFM,BFL,PFM,PFL AG	cW	cW	cW	cW	cW	cW	cW	cW
Protonotaria citrea PROTHONOTARY WARBLER[122] BFL,LA mf,ag	cT	cT	cT	cT	cT	cT		cT
Helmitheros vermivorus WORM-EATING WARBLER BFM,BFL pfm,pfl,ag	fW	fW	fW	fW	fW	fW	fW	fT
Limnothlypis swainsonii SWAINSON'S WARBLER MF,BFL	rW	rW	rW	rW	rW	X	oW	oT
Seiurus aurocapillus OVENBIRD BFM,BFL,AG	cW	cW	cW	cW	cW	cW		cW
Seiurus noveboracensis NORTHERN WATERTHRUSH MF,LA wl	cW	cW	cW	cW	cW	cW	cW	cW

Forested Habitats: BFM/bfm = submontane broadleaf forest; BFL/bfl = lowland broadleaf forest; PFM/pfm = submontane pine forest; PFL/pfl = lowland pine forest; MF/mf = mangrove and littoral forest.
Transitional Habitats: SC/sc = scrub, low second growth; SA/sa = savanna.
Unforested Habitats: AG/ag = cultivated land, pastureland, ornamental vegetation; WL/wl = wetland habitats with emergent vegetation ; LA/la = lagoons, ponds, rivers, streams; BE/be = coastal habitats; OC/oc = ocean.

Habitats	Corozal District	Orange Walk District	Belize District	Cayo District	Stann Creek District	Toledo District	Ambergris Caye	other cayes
Seiurus motacilla LOUISIANA WATERTHRUSH[123]	LA	fT	uW	fT	uW	uW	uW	uT	uT
Oporornis formosus KENTUCKY WARBLER	BFM,BFL	fW	cW	fW	cW	cW	cW	uW	cT
Oporornis philadelphia MOURNING WARBLER	SC	oT	oT	oT	oT	oT	oT	uT	uT
Geothlypis trichas COMMON YELLOWTHROAT	SC,AG,WL sa	cW	cW	cW	cW	cW	cW	cW	cW
Geothlypis poliocephala GRAY-CROWNED YELLOWTHROAT[124]	PFM,PFL,SA,SC wl	fP	cP	cP	cP	cP	lP	uP	X
Wilsonia citrina HOODED WARBLER	BFM,BFL pfm,pfl,sc	cW	cW	cW	cW	cW	cW		cW
Wilsonia pusilla WILSON'S WARBLER	BFM,BFL,AG pfm,pfl	uW	uW	uW	fW	uW	uW	oT	oT
Wilsonia canadensis CANADA WARBLER[125]	MF,AG bfl		X		X	X	oT	oT	uT
Basileuterus culicivorus GOLDEN-CROWNED WARBLER	BFM,BFL		fP	mP?	cP	cP	cP		
Basileuterus rufifrons RUFOUS-CAPPED WARBLER	PFM bfl,pfl				cP	lP	lP		
Icteria virens YELLOW-BREASTED CHAT	SC ag	fW	fW	fW	fW	fW	fW	uW	cT
Granatellus sallaei GRAY-THROATED CHAT	BFL bfm	fP	fP	uP	uP	?	rP		

COEREBIDAE (Bananaquit)								(1)
Coereba flaveola BANANAQUIT[126]	BFM,BFL,MF ag			uP	fP	fP	fP	lP	lP

THRAUPIDAE (Tanagers)								(25)
Chlorospingus ophthalmicus COMMON BUSH-TANAGER	BFM				vP	vP	vP		
Eucometis penicillata GRAY-HEADED TANAGER	BFM,BFL	?	fP	fP	fP	fP	fP		
Lanio aurantius BLACK-THROATED SHRIKE-TANAGER	BFM,BFL		fP	mP	fP	fP	fP		
Habia rubica RED-CROWNED ANT-TANAGER[127]	BFM,BFL		fP	uP	fP	fP	fP		

Key simbols:
Abundance: v = very common; c = common; f = fairly common; u = uncommon; r = rare; o = occasional; l = uncommon or even common locally, but absent or scarce in most of the district; m = marginally occurs in district.
Seasonality: P = permanent resident; S = seasonal resident only; V = visitor; T = transient; W = winter resident; X = known from only one or two records.

Species	Habitats	Corozal District	Orange Walk District	Belize District	Cayo District	Stann Creek District	Toledo District	Ambergris Caye	other cayes
Habia fuscicauda RED-THROATED ANT-TANAGER[127]	BFM,BFL / sc	vP	vP	vP	vP	vP	vP		
Piranga roseogularis ROSE-THROATED TANAGER[128]	BFL	fP	lP	lP	?				X
Piranga flava HEPATIC TANAGER	PFM,PFL			lP	cP	cP	cP		
Piranga rubra SUMMER TANAGER	BFM,BFL,PFM,PFL / AG	cW	cW	cW	cW	cW	cW	cW	cW
Piranga olivacea SCARLET TANAGER[129]	BFM,BFL,PFM,PFL	fT	uT	cT	uT	cT	cT	cT	cT
Piranga ludoviciana WESTERN TANAGER[130]	BFM,BFL,PFM,PFL / AG	X	X				X		
Piranga bidentata FLAME-COLORED TANAGER[131]	BFM					lP			
Piranga leucoptera WHITE-WINGED TANAGER	BFM / bfl,pfl			oV	fP	fP	fP		
Ramphocelus sanguinolentus CRIMSON-COLLARED TANAGER	SC			lP	lP	fP	fP		
Ramphocelus passerinii PASSERINI'S TANAGER	SC			mP	fP	cP	cP		
Thraupis episcopus BLUE-GRAY TANAGER	BFL,PFL,AG	uP	fP	cP	vP	vP	vP	rP?	
Thraupis abbas YELLOW-WINGED TANAGER	BFM,BFL,PFM,PFL / AG	?	fP	fP	cP	cP	cP		
Euphonia affinis SCRUB EUPHONIA	SC,SA,AG / bfl	fP	fP	fP	fP	uP	uP		
Euphonia hirundinacea YELLOW-THROATED EUPHONIA	BFM,BFL,PFM,PFL / AG	cP	cP	cP	cP	cP	cP		
Euphonia elegantissima ELEGANT EUPHONIA	BFM / bfl				rP	rP	rP		
Euphonia gouldi OLIVE-BACKED EUPHONIA	BFM,BFL / ag			cP	fP	cP	cP		
Euphonia minuta WHITE-VENTED EUPHONIA	BFM,BFL					rP	rP	lP	
Tangara larvata GOLDEN-HOODED TANAGER	PFM,PFL / bfm,bfl			lP	mP	fP	fP		
Chlorophanes spiza GREEN HONEYCREEPER	BFM,BFL				mP	fP	fP		
Cyanerpes lucidus SHINING HONEYCREEPER	BFM / bfl				uP	uP	uP		

Forested Habitats: BFM/bfm = submontane broadleaf forest; BFL/bfl = lowland broadleaf forest; PFM/pfm = submontane pine forest; PFL/pfl = lowland pine forest; MF/mf = mangrove and littoral forest.

Transitional Habitats: SC/sc = scrub, low second growth; SA/sa = savanna.

Unforested Habitats: AG/ag = cultivated land, pastureland, ornamental vegetation; WL/wl = wetland habitats with emergent vegetation ; LA/la = lagoons, ponds, rivers, streams; BE/be = coastal habitats; OC/oc = ocean.

Habitats	Corozal District	Orange Walk District	Belize District	Cayo District	Stann Creek District	Toledo District	Ambergris Caye	other cayes
Cyanerpes cyaneus RED-LEGGED HONEYCREEPER BFM,BFL,PFM,PFL AG	uP	cP	cP	cP	cP	cP		

EMBERIZIDAE (Seedeaters, Grassquits, and Sparrows) (21)

Habitats	Corozal District	Orange Walk District	Belize District	Cayo District	Stann Creek District	Toledo District	Ambergris Caye	other cayes
Volatinia jacarina BLUE-BLACK GRASSQUIT SC,AG,WL	cP	cP	vP	vP	vP	vP		
Sporophila schistacea SLATE-COLORED SEEDEATER[132] BFL			IP?	?		IP?		
Sporophila americana VARIABLE SEEDEATER SC,SA,AG wl		uP	cP	vP	vP	vP		
Sporophila torqueola WHITE-COLLARED SEEDEATER SC,SA,AG wl	vP	vP	vP	vP	vP	vP	[bird symbol]	IP
Oryzoborus funereus THICK-BILLED SEED-FINCH PFL,SC,SA,AG	mP	uP	cP	fP	cP	cP		
Amaurospiza concolor BLUE SEEDEATER[133] SC		X	IP					
Tiaris olivacea YELLOW-FACED GRASSQUIT[134] SC,AG		IP	IP	fP	cP	cP		
Sicalis luteola GRASSLAND YELLOW-FINCH[135] SA,AG		IP	IP	X	IP	IP		
Arremon aurantiirostris ORANGE-BILLED SPARROW BFM,BFL			mP	cP	cP	cP		
Arremonops rufivirgatus OLIVE SPARROW PFL,SA sc	cP	cP	cP	mP	mP			
Arremonops chloronotus GREEN-BACKED SPARROW BFL,SC pfl	cP	cP	cP	cP	cP	cP		
Aimophila botterii BOTTERI'S SPARROW[136] SA pfl		uP	uP	mP		X		
Aimophila rufescens RUSTY SPARROW PFM,PFL sc				IP	IP	cP		
Spizella passerina CHIPPING SPARROW PFM,PFL		fP	fP	fP	cP	cP		X
Spizella pallida CLAY-COLORED SPARROW[137] AG sc							X	
Pooecetes gramineus VESPER SPARROW[138] AG						X		
Chondestes grammacus LARK SPARROW[139] SA,AG			X				X	X
Passerculus sandwichensis SAVANNAH SPARROW AG	oW	oW	oW	oW		X	X	X

Key simbols:

Abundance: v = very common; c = common; f = fairly common; u = uncommon; r = rare; o = occasional; l = uncommon or even common locally, but absent or scarce in most of the district; m = marginally occurs in district.

Seasonality: P = permanent resident; S = seasonal resident only; V = visitor; T = transient; W = winter resident; X = known from only one or two records.

Habitats	Corozal District	Orange Walk District	Belize District	Cayo District	Stann Creek District	Toledo District	Ambergris Caye	other cayes
Ammodramus savannarum Grasshopper Sparrow[140]	SA ag		uP	cP	fP	cP	cP		X
Melospiza lincolnii Lincoln's Sparrow	SC,AG				X	X	X	oW	oT
Zonotrichia leucophrys White-crowned Sparrow[141]	SC,AG							X	

CARDINALIDAE (Saltators, Grosbeaks, and Buntings) (12)

	Habitats	Corozal District	Orange Walk District	Belize District	Cayo District	Stann Creek District	Toledo District	Ambergris Caye	other cayes
Saltator coerulescens Grayish Saltator	SC,AG		mP	fP	cP	cP	cP	cP	oV
Saltator maximus Buff-throated Saltator	BFL,AG bfm,sc			mP	fP	fP	cP	cP	?
Saltator atriceps Black-headed Saltator	BFL,AG sc	cP	cP	cP	cP	cP	cP	cP	
Caryothraustes poliogaster Black-faced Grosbeak	BFM,BFL pfm		mP	cP	lP	cP	cP	cP	
Cardinalis cardinalis Northern Cardinal	PFL,SC	fP	fP	fP	mP				
Pheucticus ludovicianus Rose-breasted Grosbeak	BFM,BFL,AG	uW	uW	uW	fW	uW	uW	uW	cT
Cyanocompsa cyanoides Blue-black Grosbeak	BFM,BFL,SC pfm,pfl		l?P	cP	fP	cP	cP	cP	
Cyanocompsa parellina Blue Bunting	BFL,SC,AG	cP	cP	fP	fP				
Guiraca caerulea Blue Grosbeak	SC,AG,WL	fW	fW	fW	fW	fW	fW	*(mark)*	cT
Passerina cyanea Indigo Bunting	SC,AG,WL	cW	cW	cW	cW	cW	cW	cW	cT
Passerina ciris Painted Bunting	SC,AG	oW	oW	oW	oW	oW	oW	uT	uT
Spiza americana Dickcissel	AG,WL sc	cT	fT	cT	fT	cT	cT	uT	uT

ICTERIDAE (Blackbirds) (19)

	Habitats	Corozal District	Orange Walk District	Belize District	Cayo District	Stann Creek District	Toledo District	Ambergris Caye	other cayes
Dolichonyx oryzivorus Bobolink	AG sc			X			X	uT	uT
Agelaius phoeniceus Red-winged Blackbird	AG,WL sc	vP	vP	vP	mP	mP			

Forested Habitats: BFM/bfm = submontane broadleaf forest; BFL/bfl = lowland broadleaf forest; PFM/pfm = submontane pine forest; PFL/pfl = lowland pine forest; MF/mf = mangrove and littoral forest.
Transitional Habitats: SC/sc = scrub, low second growth; SA/sa = savanna.
Unforested Habitats: AG/ag = cultivated land, pastureland, ornamental vegetation; WL/wl = wetland habitats with emergent vegetation ; LA/la = lagoons, ponds, rivers, streams; BE/be = coastal habitats; OC/oc = ocean.

	Habitats	Corozal District	Orange Walk District	Belize District	Cayo District	Stann Creek District	Toledo District	Ambergris Caye	other cayes
Sturnella magna EASTERN MEADOWLARK	SA,AG		cP	cP	IP	cP	cP		
Dives dives MELODIOUS BLACKBIRD	AG	vP	vP	vP	vP	vP	vP	rP?	
Quiscalus mexicanus GREAT-TAILED GRACKLE	AG,WL	vP	vP	vP	vP	vP	vP		vP
Molothrus aeneus BRONZED COWBIRD	AG	cP	fP	fP	fP	IP	IP	cP	IW
Molothrus ater BROWN-HEADED COWBIRD[142]	AG		X						
Molothrus oryzivorus GIANT COWBIRD	AG		uP	uP	uP	uP	uP		
Icterus prosthemelas BLACK-COWLED ORIOLE	BFL,PFL,SA,AG	cP	cP	cP	cP	cP	cP	IP	
Icterus spurius ORCHARD ORIOLE	SC,AG,WL	cW	cW	cW	cW	cW	cW		fT
Icterus cucullatus HOODED ORIOLE	AG	cP	fP	cP	IP	IP			IP
Icterus chrysater YELLOW-BACKED ORIOLE	PFM,PFL,AG	uP	fP	fP	cP	fP	fP	cP	
Icterus mesomelas YELLOW-TAILED ORIOLE	AG,LA	cP	fP	fP	cP	fP	uP		
Icterus auratus ORANGE ORIOLE[143]	AG	IP						uP?	
Icterus gularis ALTAMIRA ORIOLE	SC,AG	fP	uP	IP			X	uP	
Icterus galbula BALTIMORE ORIOLE	BFM,BFL,AG pfm,pfl,sc	cW	cW	cW	cW	cW	cW	cW	cT
Amblycercus holosericeus YELLOW-BILLED CACIQUE	BFL,PFL,SC	fP	cP	cP	cP	cP	cP	cP	
Psarocolius wagleri CHESTNUT-HEADED OROPENDOLA	BFL				IP	IP	IP		
Psarocolius montezuma MONTEZUMA OROPENDOLA	BFL,AG pfm	uP	cP	cP	vP	vP	vP		

FRINGILLIDAE (Finches)									(3)
Loxia curvirostra RED CROSSBILL[144]	PFM pfl		oV?	oV?	IP				
Carduelis notata BLACK-HEADED SISKIN[145]	PFM			X	cP				

Key simbols:

Abundance: v = very common; c = common; f = fairly common; u = uncommon; r = rare; o = occasional; l = uncommon or even common locally, but absent or scarce in most of the district; m = marginally occurs in district.

Seasonality: P = permanent resident; S = seasonal resident only; V = visitor; T = transient; W = winter resident; X = known from only one or two records.

	Habitats	Corozal District	Orange Walk District	Belize District	Cayo District	Stann Creek District	Toledo District	Ambergris Caye	other cayes
Carduelis psaltria LESSER GOLDFINCH[146]	AG		IP						

PASSERIDAE (Old World Sparrows)									(1)
Passer domesticus HOUSE SPARROW[147]	AG			X	oV	IP	IP		

Forested Habitats: BFM/bfm = submontane broadleaf forest; BFL/bfl = lowland broadleaf forest; PFM/pfm = submontane pine forest; PFL/pfl = lowland pine forest; MF/mf = mangrove and littoral forest.
Transitional Habitats: SC/sc = scrub, low second growth; SA/sa = savanna.
Unforested Habitats: AG/ag = cultivated land, pastureland, ornamental vegetation; WL/wl = wetland habitats with emergent vegetation ; LA/la = lagoons, ponds, rivers, streams; BE/be = coastal habitats; OC/oc = ocean.

FOOTNOTES

1 **Manx Shearwater.** Known only from a single bird picked up dead near Dangriga SC 9 Feb 1990 (Howell *et al.* 1992).

2 **Audubon's Shearwater.** One was found still alive on a beach at Caye Caulker in late Jul 2000, and another was found dead on a beach near Hopkins SC 2 Aug 2000 (Jones *et al.* 2002).

3 **White-tailed Tropicbird.** An adult was seen near Gallows Point Reef 21 Apr 1976 (Jones *et al.* 2000).

4 **Masked Booby.** Four records, all of adults: at sea off Belize City BE 15 Feb 1955 (Miller and Miller 1992); photographed on the beach at San Pedro 8 Aug 1987 (Jones *et al.* 2000); off San Pedro 13 May 1992 (Miller and Miller 1992); 6 km west of Glovers Reef 19 Dec 2000 (R. Burgos, pers. comm.).

5 **American White Pelican.** Numbers are increasing; see Jones *et al.* (2000) for a summary of records and discussion of status.

6 **Scarlet Ibis.** One was seen at Punta Ycacos Lagoon TO 17 Mar 1999 (Jones *et al.* 2002).

7 **Glossy Ibis.** *Plegadis* ibises have been seen with increasing frequency since first reported in 1969. All individuals identified to date have been *falcinellus* (see Jones *et al.* 2000 for review of records and discussion of status).

8 **Greater Flamingo.** Reported occasionally from northeast coastal Belize, but rarely documented; 2 circling over Aguacaliente Swamp TO 28 Mar 2001 (O. Figueroa, pers. comm.).

9 **Fulvous Whistling-Duck.** Numbers have increased since first reported in the mid-1980s. Most records are from Crooked Tree Wildlife Sanctuary BE (Howell *et al.* 1992; Miller and Miller 1992; Jones *et al.* 2000).

10 **Greater White-fronted Goose.** One was collected at Canton's Farm, Mile 22 on the Old Northern Highway OW, 15 Jan 1973 (Amer. Mus. Nat. Hist. specimen # 808827).

11 **Snow Goose.** Known from two records: a blue morph collected at Big Falls Farm CA/BE 23 Nov 1975 (Amer. Mus. Nat. Hist. specimen # 812017), and a white morph seen at Tres Leguas OW from 29 Jan – 12 Feb 1991 (Howell *et al.* 1992).

12 **American Wigeon.** As many as 40–50 individuals have been reported at Crooked Tree Wildlife Sanctuary BE. See Jones *et al.* (2000) for a discussion of its status.

13 **Mallard.** One was collected at Big Falls Farm CA/BE 25 Nov 1976 (Amer. Mus. Nat. Hist. specimen # 812604).

14 **Cinnamon Teal.** Six records to date (Jones *et al.* 2000). Additionally, a hybrid ♂ Cinnamon X Blue-winged Teal was seen near Belize City 19 Dec 1999 (Jones, unpubl.).

15 **Northern Shoveler.** See Jones *et al.* (2000) for a discussion of its current status.

16 **Green-winged Teal.** A rare and irregular winter visitor; there are few recent records.

17 **Ring-necked Duck.** A fairly common winter visitor at Crooked Tree Wildlife Sanctuary BE; rare elsewhere. Numbers may be increasing; see Jones *et al.* (2000) for a summary of records and status.

18 **Hooded Merganser.** A ♂ was photographed at Crooked Tree Village BE in 1990 or 1991 (Jones *et al.* 2002).

19 **Red-breasted Merganser.** One was seen 3 km north of Belize City 1 Dec 2000, and

47

2 were at Nova Shrimp Farm BE 17 Dec 2000 (Jones *et al.* 2002).

20 **Masked Duck**. One was collected at Big Falls Ranch CA 15 Mar 1975 (Amer. Mus. Nat. Hist. specimen # 824786); a ♂ was near San Antonio CA 18 Mar 1990 (Howell *et al.* 1992), and 8-12 were at Crooked Tree Wildlife Sanctuary BE 1 Feb 1997 (Jones *et al.* 2000).

21 **Mississippi Kite.** Although only recently confirmed, probably a regular but rare autumn transient (Jones *et al.* 2002).

22 **Short-tailed Hawk.** There are two reports from Caye Caulker (E. McRae and N. Smith, pers. comm.).

23 **Solitary Eagle.** Restricted to Mountain Pine Ridge and Maya Mountains. See Jones *et al.* (2000) for a discussion of its status.

24 **Crested Eagle.** Recorded from western OW and southwestern TO. See Jones *et al.* (2000) for a discussion of its status.

25 **Harpy Eagle.** Recent records are from southern CA and TO. See Jones *et al.* (2000) for discussions of its current status and unpublished data.

26 **Crested Caracara.** Several unsupported sight records but only recently documented: 1 near San Felipe OW 17 Dec 2000 (Jones *et al.* 2002).

27 **Singing Quail**. Poorly known and possibly overlooked. The first record from southern Belize (CA) is given by Howell *et al.* (1992); see also Miller and Miller (1992).

28 **Gray-breasted Crake**. See Howell *et al.* (1992) for a summary of records through 1990; recent records from TO suggest several small resident populations in the south.

29 **Yellow breasted Crake**. Recently reported (and photographed) at Crooked Tree Wildlife Sanctuary BE (Jones *et al.* 2000). Two earlier sight records: Mile 4, Western Hwy BE 27 Jun 1974 (Weyer 1974), and Big

Falls Farm CA/BE 24 May 1984 (Hecker 1984).

30 **American Golden-Plover.** A spring transient only.

31 **Collared Plover.** Breeding was recently documented at Nova Shrimp Farm BE and is suspected at other shrimp farms (Jones *et al.* 2000).

32 **Snowy Plover.** Only one confirmed record: 19 Oct 1997 at Nova Shrimp Farm BE (Jones *et al.* 2000).

33 **American Oystercatcher**. Most records are from Dangriga SC where one or two are seen almost yearly.

34 **American Avocet**. See Jones *et al.* (2000) for a summary of records and discussion of status.

35 **Upland Sandpiper**. Most records are from spring.

36 **Long-billed Curlew**. See Jones *et al.* (2000) for a summary of records and discussion of status.

37 **Hudsonian Godwit.** Two records, both during May (Jones *et al.* 2000).

38 **Marbled Godwit.** A rare autumn transient at coastal sites (Jones *et al.* 2000), with one recent winter record from Caye Caulker (J. Beveridge, pers. comm.).

39 **Semipalmated Sandpiper.** In addition to its status as a transient, a very uncommon to rare winter visitor.

40 **Western Sandpiper.** Locally common to abundant in migration.

41 **White-rumped Sandpiper.** Except for one autumn record (Jones, unpubl.), it is a spring migrant only.

42 **Dunlin.** Three confirmed records: 21 Mar 1990 near Dangriga SC (Howell *et al.* 1992); 6 Jan 1999 at Agua Mar Shrimp

Farm (Jones *et al.* 2000); 17 Dec 2000 at Nova Shrimp Farm BE (Jones, unpubl.).

43 **Long-billed Dowitcher.** A locally common winter visitor. See Jones *et al.* (2000) for a discussion of its status.

44 **Wilson's Phalarope.** Only three records, two in spring, one in autumn (Jones *et al.* 2000).

45 **Red-necked Phalarope.** An individual was seen off Caye Rosario from Nov 1993 through Jan 1994 (Jones *et al.* 2000).

46 **Great Skua.** A specimen was picked up dead on Ambergris Caye 20 Mar 1971 (Barlow *et al.* 1972). A skua sp., thought to be Great, was well seen several times around Belize City from 19 Dec 1976 until Jan 1977 (Meadows 1977).

47 **Pomarine Jaeger** and **Parasitic Jaeger.** Although adults of each have been reported with about equal frequency, the relative paucity of records, along with reports of unidentified immatures, make determination of their relative status problematical. Additional records are needed for a better understanding of their seasonal status.

48 **Laughing Gull.** Although very common in winter, its status as a breeding species in Belize has always been tenuous, with few documented nesting sites.

49 **Franklin's Gull**. See Jones *et al.* (2000) for a summary of records and discussion of status.

50 **Bonaparte's Gull**. A rare winter visitor (Jones *et al.* 2000); the most recent record was of a 1st winter bird at San Pedro, Ambergris Caye, on 26 Dec 2000 (M. Meadows, pers. comm.).

51 **Black-tailed Gull.** An adult was photographed by R. Abrams at Dangriga SC 11 Mar 1988. The photo was examined and confirmed by S. Howell (Howell and Webb 1995).

52 **Black-legged Kittiwake.** An adult was photographed at Caye Caulker 9 Jan 2000 (Jones *et al.* 2002).

53 **Common Tern.** Its seasonal status in Belize is complex and poorly understood.

54 **Forster's Tern.** A rare and irregular winter visitor. See Jones *et al.* (2000) for a summary of records and discussion of status.

55 **Black Noddy.** Historically, bred on Glovers Reef and possibly Tom Owens Caye in the Sapodilla Cayes (Russell 1964). The only recent confirmed record is that of a storm-driven individual at Belize City 31 Oct 1998 (Jones *et al.* 2000).

56 **White-crowned Pigeon.** Generally absent from the cayes in winter. Populations apparently move to adjacent mainland areas where it is occasionally reported (see Howell *et al.* 1992).

57 **Red-billed Pigeon.** Numbers have increased dramatically since it was first reported in 1960 (Russell 1964).

58 **Eurasian Collared-Dove.** Two recent records from Ambergris Caye (Jones *et al.* 2000) suggest that it may soon colonize Belize, as it has North America.

59 **White-winged Dove**. The first records of this species in Belize are given by Barlow *et al.* (1969); it is now common in the north and continuing to spread southward.

60 **Mourning Dove.** In addition to its status as a transient, it is also an occasional winter visitor.

61 **Inca Dove**. One was seen 8 Sep 1996 at Punta Gorda TO (Jones *et al.* 2000).

62 **Caribbean Dove.** Reports from mainland CO have not been confirmed.

63 **Ruddy Quail-Dove.** One was seen on Tom Owens Caye 27 May 1998 (Jones *et al.* 2000), and another on Lime Caye 1 Nov

2000, both in the Sapodilla Cayes (Jones, unpubl.).

64 **Olive-throated Parakeet.** An occasional, perhaps regular, winter visitor on Caye Caulker (McRae, Beveridge, Jones, unpubl.).

65 **Yellow-naped Parrot.** Three turned up on Calabash Caye, Turneffe Islands, shortly after Hurricane Mitch and were thought to have been transported there from the Bay Islands, Honduras, in the eye of the hurricane (Jones *et al.* 2002).

66 **Mangrove Cuckoo.** Its resident and seasonal status are still unclear.

67 **Smooth-billed Ani.** May breed occasionally on Ambergris Caye (S. Lala, pers. comm.).

68 **Burrowing Owl.** One was seen at the mouth of the Manatee River BE in Jan 1901 (Russell 1964), and another was seen 8–9 Apr 1998 near Indian Creek TO (Jones *et al.* 2000).

69 **Short-eared Owl** A mummified carcass was found at Aqua Mar Shrimp Farm TO 4 Mar 1999 (Jones *et al.* 2000).

70 **Short-tailed Nighthawk** One was seen at Cockscomb Basin SC 10 May 1998 (Jones *et al.* 2000). Additionally, one reported at South Water Caye 8 Sep 1998 (A. Case, pers. comm.), and another at Caye Caulker 25 Jan 2000 (J. Beveridge, pers. comm.) appear to be valid, suggesting that this species may be somewhat vagile.

71 **Chuck-will's-widow.** Reported in winter in CA. See Jones *et al.* (2000) for a summary of records and discussion of status.

72 **Yucatan Nightjar.** May breed locally in OW (England 2000).

73 **Whip-poor-will.** Despite very few records, it may be a regular transient and perhaps a rare winter visitor. It is nocturnal, and generally silent away from North American breeding areas.

74 **White-chinned Swift.** Rare and poorly known throughout its range. It is known in Belize from four specimens collected at Manatee Lagoon SC in 1931 (Russell 1964), and a possible sight record at Mountain Pine Ridge CA 19 Mar 1991 (Howell *et al.* 1992).

75 **Chestnut-collared Swift.** One was seen 15 Mar 1993 at Cockscomb Basin SC, and another 22 Mar 1996 at Monkey Bay Wildlife Sanctuary BE (Vallely and Aversa 1997).

76 **Brown Violet-ear.** Two extralimital records: one from the vicinity of Manatee Lagoon BE 28 Jul 1905, and another from Hill Bank OW 25 Nov 1956 (both Russell 1964).

77 **Violet-crowned Woodnymph.** One (extralimital?) record from the Mountain Pine Ridge CA 22 Nov 1999 (J. Rowlett and M. Edwards, pers. comm.).

78 **Blue-throated Goldentail.** One was seen 55 km west of Belize City (in CA) 19 Apr 1987 (Mills and Rogers 1988), and another was near San Pedro Columbia TO 3 Apr 1994 (Vallely and Aversa 1997).

79 **Purple-crowned Fairy.** One extralimital record from Caye Caulker 15 Aug 1999 (J. Beveridge, pers. comm.).

80 **Long-billed Starthroat.** Three records, all recent: one at Mile 40 Western Highway CA 21 Sep 1999, one at Big Falls TO 29 Jul 2000, and two 11 km south of La Democracia BE 24 May 2001 (Jones *et al.* 2002)

81 **Black-headed Trogon.** Occasionally seen on Caye Caulker in winter (E. McRae and P. Balderamos, pers. comm.).

82 **Green Kingfisher.** Recorded twice on Ambergris Caye, 21 Sep 1998 and 18 Mar 1999 (S. Lala, pers. comm.).

83 **American Pygmy Kingfisher.** One seen and photographed on Caye Caulker 29 Mar to 28 Apr 2000 (J. Beveridge, pers. comm.).

84 **Scaly-throated Foliage-gleaner.** Recorded only from Doyle's Delight CA/TO

where it is apparently resident (Howell *et al.* 1992; Miller and Miller 1992).

85 **Tawny-throated Leaftosser**. Replaces *S. guatemalensis* on the higher ridges of the Maya Mountains. See Jones *et al.* (2000) for a summary of records and discussion of status.

86 **Slaty Antwren**. Recorded from Union Camp, Columbia Forest Reserve TO (Parker et. al 1993), Doyle's Delight CA/TO (Matola 1995), and near Little Quartz Ridge TO. See Jones *et al.* (2000) for a summary of records and discussion of status.

87 **Caribbean Elaenia.** A rare winter visitor to the cayes, with breeding documented only on Caye Caulker (Howell *et al.* 1992; Jones, unpubl.). It may also breed occasionally on Ambergris Caye. Most records from the mainland are undocumented.

88 **Yellow-bellied Elaenia.** Occasionally seen on Caye Caulker (E. McRae, pers. comm.); also seen on Seal Caye in the Sapodilla Cayes 9 Nov 2000 (Jones, unpubl.).

89 **Paltry Tyrannulet**. In Belize it is restricted to southern TO. See Jones *et al.* (2000) for a summary of records and discussion of status.

90 **Olive-sided Flycatcher.** It is also a fairly common winter visitor at higher elevations in the Maya Mountains.

91 **Western Wood-Pewee**. Two were seen and heard in the Mountain Pine Ridge CA 25 Oct 1998 (Jones *et al.* 2000).

92 **Alder Flycatcher.** Its status in spring is unclear, with no fully documented spring records. Its status in the northern half of the mainland is also unclear.

93 **Willow Flycatcher.** Its status in the northern half of the mainland is unclear; it is probably overlooked.

94 **White-throated Flycatcher**. Its status in Belize is poorly understood. It may be a local winter visitor in brushy vegetation bordering freshwater marshes. Definitely recorded only from Hill Bank OW (Vallely and Whitman 1997), Gallon Jug OW (Miller and Miller 1992), and Columbia River Forest Station TO (Wood and Leberman 1987).

95 **Brown-crested Flycatcher.** Contrary to the published literature, popular checklists, and Christmas Bird Counts, this species is migratory in Belize, with relatively few documented winter records (Jones, unpubl.).

96 **Great Kiskadee.** Occurs regularly in winter on Caye Caulker (E. McRae and J. Beveridge, pers. comm.).

97 **Cassin's Kingbird.** Despite a number of published accounts, there is only one confirmed record: Gallon Jug OW, 22 Dec 1999 – 2 Mar 2000 (Lasley *et al.* 2001).

98 **Gray Kingbird**. Most records are from the northern cayes and mainland coast during spring (mostly mid-Mar to mid-May). See Jones *et al.* (2000) for a summary of records and discussion of status.

99 **Scissor-tailed Flycatcher**. A fairly common transient and local winter visitor. See Jones *et al.* (2000) for a summary of records and discussion of status.

100 **White-winged Becard**. Has slowly spread northward since it was first documented in southern TO in 1970. See Jones *et al.* (2000) for a summary of records and discussion of status.

101 **Plumbeous Vireo.** The taxonomic affinities of the resident populations in Belize are unclear, but they seem closest to *Vireo plumbeus* from the mountains of Mexico and Central America. There are three disjunct populations in Belize: one in pines and broadleaf forest in and near the Mountain Pine Ridge CA, another in open pine woodlands east of the Cockscomb Basin SC, and a third in broadleaf forest at higher elevations in the Maya Mountains (Jones, unpubl.).

102 **Blue-headed Vireo.** One was seen 25–26 Dec 2000 in Belmopan (Jones *et al.* 2002).

103 **Warbling Vireo.** Two convincing records: one at Union Camp TO 4 Apr 1992 (Parker *et al.* 1993), and one at Crooked Tree Village BE 21 Mar 1999 (P. and A. Rodewald, pers. comm.). There are at least two other probable records.

104 **Black-whiskered Vireo.** One was found dead on Half Moon Caye 22 Mar 1926 (Russell 1964).

105 **Snowy-bellied Martin.** Several Caribbean or Sinaloa Martins were seen by B. Monroe in late Aug 1962 flying out to sea from Belize City with Purple Martins (Howell and Webb 1995). As these two "species" are nearly impossible to tell apart in the field (and considered by some to be conspecific), the record is treated here as the combined form known as Snowy-bellied Martin.

106 **Gray-breasted Martin.** A seasonal resident only (Jan–Sep); not present year-round as commonly believed. See Jones *et al.* (2000) for a discussion of its seasonal occurrence in Belize.

107 **Northern Rough-winged Swallow.** Both northern migrant forms and resident breeding populations occur in Belize. One of the resident forms *ridgwayi* (recorded from BE, CA, SC, and TO), has been treated as specifically distinct (Phillips 1986; Howell and Webb 1995).

108 **Cave Swallow.** A scarce migrant, with recent records of both the northern form *P. f. pallida* and the Yucatan form *P. f.* citata (see Jones *et al.* 2000).

109 **Carolina Wren.** Found at a few widely scattered locations in low stature forest in OW and CA. The form found in the Yucatan Peninsula, including Belize, is sometimes treated as a separate species, the White-browed Wren *T. albinucha* (Phillips 1986).

110 **Sedge Wren.** The subspecies *russelli* is endemic to Belize.

111 **Blue-gray Gnatcatcher.** Both resident and northern migrant populations are found in Belize.

112 **American Robin.** One was seen at Hill Bank OW 5 Jan 1981 (Meadows 1981).

113 **Nashville Warbler**. An occasional transient and rare winter visitor (Jones *et al.* 2000). The only subspecies documented from Belize is the western *V. r. ridgwayi*.

114 **Virginia's Warbler**. Very few documented records (Jones *et al.* 2000).

115 **Tropical Parula**. Recorded only from the Vaca Plateau CA and the Maya Mountains. See Jones *et al.* (2000) for a summary of records and discussion of status.

116 **Yellow Warbler.** Both northern migrant and resident populations occur. The resident Mangrove Warbler (*D. p. erithachorides*) is confined to mangrove forests along the coast and throughout the cayes where it is common.

117 **Yellow-rumped Warbler.** The "Myrtle" Warbler (*D. c. coronata*) is the form typically found in Belize; however, the distinctive "Audubon's" Warbler (*D. c. audubonii*) has been reported on at least one occasion (Jones, unpubl.).

118 **Black-throated Gray Warbler**. A ♂ was seen 1 Apr 1990 at Ambergris Caye (Jones *et al.* 2000).

119 **Hermit Warbler.** Three records, all ♂: one was seen 28 Dec 1991 at Bermudian Landing BE, and another was seen 23 Mar 2000 at Thousand Foot Falls, Mountain Pine Ridge CA (Barnett and Kirwan 2000). Interestingly, one was seen again at Thousand Foot Falls 20 Feb 2001 and is thought to have been the same individual (G. Crawford, pers. comm.).

120 **Blackpoll Warbler.** A rare spring transient, with only one believable fall record. See Jones *et al.* (2000) for a summary of records and discussion of status.

121 **Cerulean Warbler.** Apparently a common spring migrant in the Maya Mountains. Parker (1994) suggested that a significant portion of the total population of this relatively rare wood warbler may migrate through the Maya Mountains in spring. Away from the Maya Mountains, it is a very uncommon spring and autumn transient.

122 **Prothonotary Warbler.** It is significantly more common in autumn than in spring. There are few documented winter records.

123 **Louisiana Waterthrush.** Largely confined to the interior in winter; elsewhere it occurs principally as a transient.

124 **Gray-crowned Yellowthroat.** One was on Caye Caulker 3 Oct 2000 following Hurricane Keith (E. McRae, pers. comm.).

125 **Canada Warbler.** An occasional fall transient, primarily in the cayes; rare in spring. See Jones *et al.* (2000) for a summary of records and discussion of status.

126 **Bananaquit.** Two distinctive subspecies occur in Belize, *C. f. caboti* on Ambergris Caye and Caye Caulker, and *C. f. mexicana* on the mainland south of OW and central BE (Jones *et al.* 2000).

127 **Red-crowned Ant-Tanager.** This species is increasingly common inland and at higher elevations, and outnumbers **Red-throated Ant-Tanager** at higher elevations. It is scarce or absent in most coastal areas.

128 **Rose-throated Tanager.** There is one record from Shipstern Caye, about 1 km off the mainland coast (Jones, unpubl.).

129 **Scarlet Tanager.** One winter record: a ♂ with an injured wing near Sandhill BE on 19 Dec 1999 (Jones, unpubl.).

130 **Western Tanager.** Undoubtedly occurs in Belize, but there are apparently only 2 records with both a date *and* locality, and none have been adequately documented.

131 **Flame-colored Tanager.** A small resident population was discovered at the summit of Mt. Margaret SC in 1994 (Jones *et al.* 2000).

132 **Slate-colored Seedeater**. Nomadic. Increasingly reported since it was first discovered in Belize in 1989 (Howell *et al.* (1992). It is generally not resident in any one area for long periods. In Belize, it does not appear to associate closely with bamboo as suggested in the literature (Jones, pers. observations).

133 **Blue Seedeater**. This normally mid- to high-elevation species has been found recently in bamboo thickets at Monkey Bay Wildlife Sanctuary BE and in the vicinity of Bermudian Landing BE (Howell *et al.* 1992; Vallely and Aversa 1997) where it appears to be resident.

134 **Yellow-faced Grassquit.** This forest edge and second growth species has expanded rapidly through much of Belize since it was first recorded in the late 1970s or early 1980s.

135 **Grassland Yellow-Finch**. One collected at Mussel Creek BE 10 Oct 1971 (Wood and Leberman 1987) was the first record for Belize. Small isolated populations have been found elsewhere in Belize in recent years (Vallely and Aversa 1997; Jones, unpubl.; O. Figueroa, pers. comm.) These may represent a recent and rapid range expansion or, more likely, previously overlooked populations.

136 **Botteri's Sparrow.** Two birds collected in northeastern TO 19 Jun 1963 (Russell 1964) remain the only record for southern Belize despite several recent searches of the area in different seasons.

137 **Clay-colored Sparrow**. Two records, both from Ambergris Caye in fall 1996: one on 25 Sep 8 km north of San Pedro and another on 21–22 Oct south of San Pedro (Jones *et al.* (2000).

138 **Vesper Sparrow.** One was seen near Punta Gorda 26 Aug 2001 (Jones et al. 2002).

53

139 **Lark Sparrow**. Five documented records (Kamstra 1986; Jones *et al.* 2000; M. Muschamp, pers. comm.).

140 **Grasshopper Sparrow**. Both resident (*A. s. cracens*) and migrant populations from North America are found in Belize, although migrants are seldom recorded.

141 **White-crowned Sparrow**. One was seen on Ambergris Caye 28 Oct 1988 (Howell *et al.* 1992).

142 **Brown-headed Cowbird.** A ♀ was seen with Bronzed Cowbirds at Gallon Jug OW 1 Mar 2000 (Jones *et al.* 2002).

143 **Orange Oriole.** There is a small resident population in northeastern CO. It is recorded primarily in winter on Ambergris Caye, where breeding has not been confirmed.

144 **Red Crossbill**. An uncommon resident in the Mountain Pine Ridge CA; recorded twice in lowland pine woods near Hill Bank OW (Russell 1964) and near the Belize Zoo at Mile 29 Western Highway BE.

145 **Black-headed Siskin.** One lowland record: 1 at Monkey Bay Wildlife Sanctuary BE 28 Feb 2001 (M. Haldeman, pers. comm.).

146 **Lesser Goldfinch.** Several recent records from ne OW suggest that a small resident population may be established (Jones *et al.* 2002).

147 **House Sparrow.** Well established in Punta Gorda TO and recently established in Dangriga and Pomona SC.

SPECIES OF CONCERN

BirdLife International (2000) has published a comprehensive compendium of globally threatened birds based on many years of monitoring and research. Although Belize is not one of the critical endemic bird areas of the world (Stattersfield *et al.* 1998), it does harbor a few species that are globally threatened or near threatened. These are discussed briefly below.

GLOBALLY ENDANGERED   (1)

Yellow-headed Parrot *Amazona oratrix*
This species is found locally in Mexico, in Belize, and marginally in northwest Honduras, with two records from Guatemala. It is listed as endangered because many thousands are still exported for the pet trade annually, principally from Mexico. Although hunted and persecuted in Belize both for the pet trade and because of alleged crop damage, it is still fairly common and widespread in its pine savanna habitat. A number of authors have noted its decline in Belize since the 1970s; however, the notion that it "is now primarily restricted to central and northwest areas" (BirdLife International 2000) is unfounded. The distinctive subspecies *belizensis* is virtually endemic. Continuing educational programs in the schools and media, along with increased law enforcement, are necessary for its continued survival in the wild.

GLOBALLY VULNERABLE   (1)

Keel-billed Motmot *Electron carinatum*
This species was found from southern Mexico to Costa Rica but has been extirpated from many areas, and it may now be extinct in Mexico. It requires unfragmented tracts of primary rainforest. Its distribution is very patchy, and it is generally rare where it is found. It is listed as vulnerable because of continued widespread and rapid destruction of its rainforest habitat. While seriously threatened within its restricted range in other Central American countries, it is still fairly common locally in the southern half of Belize,

principally in the Maya Mountains and the Vaca Plateau. Continued protection in Belize, where much of its habitat is in preserves, may be its only realistic hope for global survival if habitat conversion continues at its present pace in other Central American countries.

GLOBALLY NEAR THREATENED   (6)

Crested Eagle *Morphnus guianensis*
This species has an extensive range in lowland forests from northern Central America to Bolivia and Argentina; however, it is very sparsely distributed and occurs in low densities where it is found. There are few documented records in Belize, where it was not discovered until 1990. Some old reports of Harpy Eagle may also pertain to this species. From the few records to date, it appears to be restricted to western OW and southwest TO (Miller and Miller 1992; Jones *et al.* 2000). Its breeding requirements are similar to those of the Harpy Eagle, requiring large tracts of unbroken primary rainforest. Its ultimate survival is thus dependent on the preservation of extensive areas of forest.

Harpy Eagle *Harpia harpyja*
Like the preceding species, the Harpy Eagle is sparsely distributed and rare throughout its range, which extends from southern Mexico to Argentina. It requires a large breeding territory within mature lowland tropical forests. As a result of extensive forest clearing, it has been extirpated from much of its original Central American range. In Belize it has been recorded on very few occasions, and most old records are suspect. Recent records are from southern CA and TO (Jones *et al.* 2000; Whitacre *et al.* in press) where it is probably a rare breeding resident. Sufficiently large tracts of suitable forest habitat are the limiting factor in this species' breeding success.

Great Curassow *Crax rubra*
This species is found in undisturbed moist tropical forests from Mexico to Colombia. Because

of extensive forest destruction, its population centers are now highly fragmented. Additionally, hunting pressure has severely reduced its numbers within the few areas where undisturbed forest remains. Belize, incidentally, is the only country where it is still legally hunted. Because it does quite well in areas where it is protected from hunting, the creation of several large preserves in Belize has prevented the widespread population losses seen in other countries.

Ocellated Turkey *Melleagris ocellata*
This Yucatan endemic has a small global distribution. Like the preceding three species, it is a forest dweller, and its principal cause of decline has been large-scale forest destruction. Like the curassow, it does not fare well in areas subjected to intensive hunting pressure. In Belize it is restricted to the western portion of the country where, fortunately, much of its forest habitat has been protected in both public and private reserves.

Black Rail *Laterallus jamaicensis*
This little known, highly secretive marsh species is widespread throughout much of North and South America, but its population centers are, for the most part, small and widely separated, and it is absent from many areas of apparently suitable habitat. It inhabits the short-grass fringes of marshes which are highly susceptible to grazing and agricultural expansion. Its status in Belize is poorly understood—there are only four records—but two birds collected in late June (Russell 1964) suggest that it may be a rare and local resident rather than a vagrant.

Black Catbird *Melanoptila glabrirostris*
This species has a very limited global distribution, being restricted to scrubby woodland in the Yucatan Peninsula, principally along the coast and on islands, but also in limited numbers well inland. Its principal threats are unrestricted development, especially for tourist resorts, and conversion of its habitat to various agricultural uses. In Belize, it is common on Ambergris Caye and Caye Caulker but is no longer found on Lighthouse Reef and Glovers Reef where it formerly occurred (Russell 1964). It is also found locally on the mainland west to eastern OW and south to central BE. Because bird populations on cayes are highly vulnerable to hurricanes,

development, and other factors, even common birds on small cayes are not secure.

THREATENED IN BELIZE
BUT NOT GLOBALLY   (9)

In addition to those species identified as globally endangered, vulnerable, or near threatened by BirdLife International, several others are threatened with extinction in Belize. The species listed below were either formerly more common and widespread in Belize than presently, or they have always been rare and presently cling to a precarious existence within the country.

Solitary Eagle *Harpyhaliaetus solitarius*
Although only recently confirmed from Belize (Jones *et al.* 2000), substantial information (largely anecdotal) suggests that it is a rare resident in the Mountain Pine Ridge and Maya Mountains. If it does breed in Belize, the number of breeding pairs must be very small. This species requires large tracts of unbroken primary forest for successful nesting.

Ornate Hawk-Eagle *Spizaetus ornatus*
This species is noticeably less common than formerly, probably due to rainforest destruction and illegal shooting.

Orange-breasted Falcon *Falco deiroleucus*
There are only four known aeries in Belize. It too requires unbroken primary forest for survival.

Sandwich Tern *Sterna sandvicensis*
Although common in winter, it has been nearly extirpated as a breeding species in Belize by development and other indiscriminate uses of the cayes.

Roseate Tern *Sterna dougallii*
While widespread throughout much of the North Temperate and Tropical zones, it is nowhere especially common. It has been nearly exterminated as a breeding species in Belize. Little information is available on current nesting colonies.

Bridled Tern *Sterna anaethetus*
The breeding population in Belize has declined significantly due to unregulated development and other uses of the cayes where it breeds.

Sooty Tern *Sterna fuscata*
This species is suffering dramatic declines throughout much of its pantropical range. Although apparently never common in Belize (Russell 1964); it may now be reduced to one small colony on Middle Snake Caye TO, which is not adequately protected from poachers and their pets.

Brown Noddy *Anous stolidus*
Apparently extirpated as a breeding species in Belize following indiscriminate development and infestation of its former nesting sites with an assortment of feral animals.

Scarlet Macaw *Ara macao*
Like many other species of parrots that are exploited for the pet trade, the Scarlet Macaw has suffered extensive population declines and local extinctions throughout much of its range in Central and South America. However, sufficiently large populations still exist in some areas that, on a global basis, it is not yet considered threatened. Its range in Belize is restricted almost entirely to southern CA where it breeds, and western SC where it may be only seasonal. It is still hunted in Belize for food; however, few birds in Belize are taken for the pet trade.

WATCH LIST   (3)

These species are not currently threatened in Belize but could become threatened in the future if inadequately protected from illegal hunting, poaching, or habitat destruction.

Jabiru *Jabiru mycteria*
This species is more common now than 20 years ago, the result of habitat protection in conjunction with public awareness programs, especially through efforts of the Belize Audubon Society. Until recently, it was thought to leave Belize outside of the nesting season for Mexico where it is not adequately protected. Now that its foraging and nesting habitats have been preserved, especially in and around the Crooked Tree Wildlife Sanctuary, it has become a year-round resident. Considerable additional foraging habitat has been created with the proliferation of ricefields and shrimp farms in the past 20 years.

Muscovy Duck *Cairina moschata*
This species is not hunted in Belize as vigorously as in some neighboring countries. Much suitable habitat remains, so it is still relatively common in many areas.

Crested Guan *Penelope purpurascens*
Although legally hunted in Belize, it is currently protected in several large tracts of unbroken forest. It is less common generally than the Great Curassow, perhaps because of its conspicuous nature of foraging in trees where it is more easily taken by hunters.

BIBLIOGRAPHY

American Ornithologists' Union. 1998. *The A. O. U. check-list of North American birds.* 7th ed. The Allen Press, Lawrence, KS.

American Ornithologists' Union. 2000. 42nd supplement to the A. O. U. check-list of North American birds. *Auk* 117: 847- 858.

Barlow, J. C., Dick, J. A., Baldwin, D. H., and Davis, R. A. 1969. New records of birds from British Honduras. *Ibis* 111:399-402.

Barlow, J. C., Dick, J. A., Weyer, D., and Young, W. F. 1972. New records of birds from British Honduras (Belize) including a Skua. *Condor* 74: 486-487.

Barnett, J. M., and Kirwan, G. M. 2000. Neotropical notebook. *Cotinga* 14:106.

BirdLife International. 2000. *Threatened birds of the world.* Barcelona and Cambridge, UK: Lynx Edicions and BirdLife International.

England, M. 2000. The landbird monitoring programme at Lamanai, Belize: a preliminary assessment. *Cotinga* 13:32-43.

Garcia, J., Matola, S., Meadows, M., and Wright, C. 1994. *A Checklist of the Birds of Belize.* World Wildlife Fund.

Hecker, S. 1984. An invitation to look for rails at Big Falls Ranch. *Belize Audubon Soc. Newsl.* 16(4):1-2.

Howell, S. N. G., Dowell, B. A., James, D. A., Behrstock, R. A., and Robbins, C. S. 1992. New and noteworthy bird records from Belize. *Bull. Brit. Ornith. Club* 112: 235-244.

Howell, S. N. G., and Webb, S. 1995. *A guide to the birds of Mexico and northern Central America.* Oxford University Press.

Jones, H. L. 2002. Erroneous and unconfirmed bird reports from Belize: setting the record straight. *Bull. Brit. Ornith. Club* (in press).

Jones, H. L., McRae, E., Meadows, M., and Howell, S. N.G. 2000. Status updates for selected bird species in Belize, including several species previously undocumented from the country. *Cotinga* 13:17-31.

Jones, H. L., Balderamos, P., Crawford, G., Caulfield, J. and A., Donegan, T. M., McRae, E., Meadows, M., Muschamp, M., Rodriguez, T., Urbina, J., Saqui, van der Spek, V., and Zimmer, B. 2002. Fourteen new bird species reported from Belize. *Cotinga* 17 (in press).

Kamstra, J. 1986. Lark Sparrow near Belize City. *Belize Audubon Soc. Newsl.* 17(11):8.

Lasley, G. W., Miller, B. W., and Miller, C. M. 2001. Cassin's Kingbird *Tyrannus vociferans* documented in Belize. *Cotinga* 15:60-61.

Meadows, M. 1977. Great Skua sighted off Belize City. *Belize Audubon Soc. Newsl.* 8 (1):5-6.

Meadows, M. 1981. Unusual sightings 1981. *Belize Audubon Soc. Newsl.* 12 (10):4-5.

Miller, B. W., and Miller, C. M. 1992. Distributional notes and new species records for birds in Belize. *Occas. Papers Belize Nat. Hist. Soc.* 1:6-25.

Miller, B. W., and Miller, C. M. 1996. New information on the status and distribution of the Keel-billed Motmot *Electron carinatum* in Belize, Central America. *Cotinga* 6: 61-64.

Miller, B. W., and Miller, C. M. 1998. *Birds of Belize: a checklist.* Belize Audubon Society.

Miller, B. W., and Miller, C. M. 2000. *Birds of Belize: a checklist*, 2nd revised edition. Belize Audubon Society.

Mills, E. D., and Rogers, D. T. 1988. First record of the Blue-throated Golden-tail (*Hylocharis Eliciae*) in Belize. *Wilson Bull.* 100 (3): 510

Parker, T. A., Holst, B. K., Emmons, L. H., and Meyer, J. R. 1993. *A biological assessment of the Columbia River Forest Reserve, Toledo District, Belize.* RAP Working Papers 3, Conservation International Washington, DC.

Parker, T. A. 1994. Habitat, behavior and spring migration of Cerulean Warbler in Belize. *Amer. Birds* 48 (1):70-75.

Phillips, A .R. 1986. *The known birds of North and Middle America, Part 1.* A. R. Phillips, Denver, CO.

Russell, S. M. 1964. A distributional study of the birds of British Honduras. *Ornith. Monographs* No. 1, American Ornithologists' Union.

Stattersfield, A. J., Crosby, M. J., Long, A. J., and Wege, D. C. 1998. *Endemic bird areas of the world: priorities for bird conservation.* Cambridge, UK: BirdLife International (BirdLife Conservation Series 7).

Vallely, A. C., and Aversa, T. 1997. New and noteworthy bird records from Belize, including the first record of Chestnut-collared Swift *Cypseloides rutilus. Bull. Brit. Ornith. Club* 117 (4):272-274.

Vallely, A. C., and Whitman, A. A. 1997. The birds of Hill Bank, northern Belize. *Cotinga* 8 :39-49.

Weyer, D. 1974. New and interesting recent sightings. *Belize Audubon Soc. Newsl.* 6 (5):1-2.

Wood, D. S., and Leberman, R. C. 1987. Results of the Carnegie Museum of Natural History expeditions to Belize: distributional notes on the birds of Belize. *Annals Carnegie Mus.* 56:137-160.

Wood, D. S., Leberman, R. C., and Weyer D. 1986. Checklist of the birds of Belize. *Carnegie Museum Special Publication no.12.*

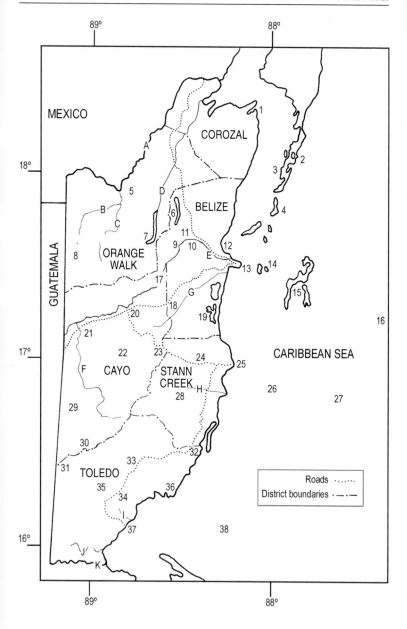

LOCALITIES MENTIONED IN FOOTNOTES

1   Shipstern Caye
2   Ambergris Caye
3   Cayo Rosario
4   Caye Caulker
5   San Felipe
6   Crooked Tree
7   Hill Bank
8   Gallon Jug
9   Bermudian Landing
10 Mussel Creek
11 Sandhill
12 Nova Shrimp Farm
13 Belize City
14 Gallows Point Reef
15 Turneffe Islands
16 Half Moon Caye
17 Big Falls Farm
18 Monkey Bay
19 Manatee Lagoon
20 Belmopan
21 San Antonio
22 Mountain Pine Ridge
23 Mt. Margaret
24 Pomona
25 Dangriga
26 South Water Caye
27 Glover's Reef
28 Cockscomb Basin
29 Vaca Plateau
30 Doyle's Delight
31 Union Camp/Little Quartz Ridge
32 Aqua Mar Shrimp Farm
33 Indian Creek Village
34 Big Falls, Toledo
35 San Pedro Columbia
36 Punta Ycacos Lagoon
37 Punta Gorda
38 Sapodilla Cayes

RIVERS

A   Rio Hondo
B   Rio Bravo
C   Booth's River
D   New River
E   Belize River
F   Macal River
G   Sibun River
H   Sittee River
I   Rio Grande
J   Temash River
K   Sarstoon River

INDEX

69

Other titles available:

- **On Observar Ocells a Catalunya** (14 authors) *Text in Catalan*
- **Where to Watch Birds in Catalonia** (14 authors) *Text in English*
- **Els Ocells del P.N. dels Aiguamolls de l'Empordà** (J. Sargatal and J. del Hoyo; colour drawings by F. Jutglar) *Text in Catalan*
- **Els Ocells del Delta de l'Ebre** (A. Martínez Vilalta and A. Motis; colour drawings by F. Jutglar) *Text in Catalan*
- **Las Aves de Doñana** (C. Llandres and C. Urdiales; colour drawings by F. Jutglar) *Text in Spanish*
- **Las Aves del P.N. de Las Tablas de Daimiel y Otros Humedales Manchegos** (J. Jiménez García-Herrera, A. del Moral, C. Morillo and M.J. Sánchez; colour drawings by F. Jutglar) *Text in Spanish*
- **Els Ocells del Delta del Llobregat** (R. Gutiérrez, P. Esteban and F.X. Santaeufemia; colour drawings by F. Jutglar) *Text in Catalan*
- **Les Oiseaux de la Camargue** (J. Boutin; colour drawings by F. Jutglar) *Text in French*
- **La Fauna del Parc Natural del Cadí-Moixerò** (J. García Petit) *Text in Catalan*
- **Los Señores del Bosque -Conservación del lobo, el lince, el oso y el bisonte en Europa** (Ch. Kempf) *Text in Spanish*
- **Els Ocells d'Osona** (17 authors) *Text in Catalan*
- **Dónde Observar Aves en España** (Sociedad Española de Ornitología -SEO-, coordinated by E. de Juana) *Text in Spanish*
- **Where to Watch Birds in Spain** (Sociedad Española de Ornitología -SEO-, coordinated by E. de Juana) *Text in English*
- **Alimentación Sana -Combinar placer y salud-** (J. del Hoyo) *Text in Spanish*
- **Castells y Castellers -Guia completa del món casteller-** (X. Brotons) *Text in Catalan*
- **Els Grans Mamífers de Catalunya i Andorra** (J. Ruiz-Olmo and À. Aguilar) *Text in Catalan*
- **Terra de Gantes -Història dels Aiguamolls de l'Empordà segons la cigonya Guita-** (5 authors; colour drawings by T. Llobet) *Text in Catalan*
- **Las Aves Marinas de España y Portugal** (A. Paterson) *Text in Spanish*
- **Atlas de las Aves de España −1975/1995−** (Sociedad Española de Ornitología -SEO-) *Text in Spanish*
- **La Fauna Vertebrada d'Osona** (J. Baucells, J. Camprodón and M. Ordeix) *Text in Catalan*
- **Veus d'ocells** (C. Fonoll, includes a CD with bird songs edited by E. Matheu) *Text in Catalan*
- **Guía de las Aves de España. Península, Baleares y Canarias** (E. de Juana, drawings by J. Varela) *Text in Spanish*
- **Threatened Birds of the World** (BirdLife International) *Text in English*
- **Els Ocells del Vallès Oriental** (J. Ribas) *Text in Catalan*
- **Flora y Fauna de España y del Mediterráneo** (P. Sterry) *Text in Spanish*
- **Lista Comentada de las Aves Argentinas/Annotated Checklist of the Birds of Argentina** (J. Mazar Barnett and M. Pearman) *Text in Spanish and English*
- **Guía Sonora de las Aves de Europa** (J. C. Roché and J. Chevereau) *Text in Spanish*
- **The Spanish Imperial Eagle** (M. Ferrer) *Text in English*
- **Grebes of our World** (A. Konter) *Text in English*
- **Handbook of the Birds of the World, Volume 1** (J. del Hoyo, A. Elliott and J. Sargatal) *Text in English*
- **Handbook of the Birds of the World, Volume 2** (J. del Hoyo, A. Elliott and J. Sargatal) *Text in English*
- **Handbook of the Birds of the World, Volume 3** (J. del Hoyo, A. Elliott and J. Sargatal) *Text in English*
- **Handbook of the Birds of the World, Volume 4** (J. del Hoyo, A. Elliott and J. Sargatal) *Text in English*
- **Handbook of the Birds of the World, Volume 5** (J. del Hoyo, A. Elliott and J. Sargatal) *Text in English*
- **Handbook of the Birds of the World, Volume 6** (J. del Hoyo, A. Elliott and J. Sargatal) *Text in English*

Lynx Edicions, Passeig de Gràcia, 12, E-08007-Barcelona, Spain.
Tel: +34 93 301 07 77   *Fax*: +34 93 302 14 75.
E-mail: lynx@hbw.com   *Web*: www.hbw.com